BUNNER'S

BUNNER'S

Simple & Delicious
Gluten-Free Vegan Treats

WRITTEN AND PHOTOGRAPHED BY

ASHLEY WITTIG & KEVIN MACALLISTER

Collins

Published by Collins, an imprint of HarperCollins Publishers Ltd

First edition

HarperCollins books may be purchased for educational, business,
or sales promotional use through our Special Markets Department.

HarperCollins Publishers Ltd
2 Bloor Street East, 20th Floor
Toronto, Ontario, Canada, M4W 1A8

www.harpercollins.ca

Library and Archives Canada Cataloguing in Publication
information is available upon request

ISBN 978-1-44343-239-9

Printed and bound in Canada
TC 9 8 7 6 5 4 3 2 1

To animal rights advocates everywhere, for their tireless efforts in the promotion of respect and compassion for all living things

CONTENTS

Introduction 1

Pantry Primer 7

Breakfast of Champions 21

Muffins.. 43

Savouries... 65

Cookies, Bars & Squares.............................. 87

Donuts...113

Cakes..125

Cupcakes...149

Sweet Pies & Tarts 167

Holiday...189

Frostings & Toppings 217

Acknowledgements 247

Index 251

INTRODUCTION

I have always been a great eater. My parents' nickname for me as a kid was "Wilf," after my amazing but insatiable grandfather, who would eat the free butter at a restaurant as if it were an appetizer. But it wasn't the savoury or salty snacks that called me; my obsession was the sweet treats. From the first moments I was old enough to reach them, I've been shooed away from trays of cooling cookies and told not to hover around dessert tables. To say that I have a sweet tooth is probably an understatement.

As a little girl I learned to make my own treats. I insisted on following each recipe to the letter, never letting my mother, a chef, derail me with her ad-libbed flourishes and wayward measurements. In high school I baked my friends muffins and cookies and delivered them in hand-decorated paper bags. Even in university, when my focus should have been on passing my next exam, I found myself deeply enthralled in the dessert chapters of cookbooks, daydreaming about all things glazed and frosted. Although at the time I couldn't see where I was headed, in retrospect it's clear that I was meant to be a baker.

But about five years ago, my love affair with all things butter, eggs, and sugar changed. To gear myself up for a 30-day "vegan challenge" I was undertaking for my job as sales director for a natural cosmetics company, I watched a video on the PETA website called "Meet Your Meat" that completely changed my perspective on what was on my plate and in my mixing bowl. As someone who formerly ate her steaks blue rare and practically lived off Buffalo chicken fingers, becoming an overnight vegan was a pretty drastic change. At first I couldn't see how any of the foods I loved would fit into my new lifestyle—without dairy or eggs, baking cakes and cookies seemed impossible. But as the weeks passed, I began to adjust, and my love of food meant I was unwilling to just give up on the things I loved to eat.

I found myself deeply enthralled in the dessert chapters of cookbooks, daydreaming about all things glazed and frosted. Although at the time I couldn't see where I was headed, in retrospect it's clear that I was meant to be a baker.

So I began to experiment with new recipes and new techniques and soon was thriving on my new diet.

Around that same time, another major change happened in my life. I met Kevin at a work function (we worked for the same company) and sparks flew. We were instantly inseparable, and in the way that new couples do, we quickly had nicknames for each other. I called him Kev (boring, I know!), and he started calling me Bunner because, as he puts it, I look "like a bun."

Our jobs at the time had us traversing Canada, the United States, and sometimes Europe, which had been fun when we were both single, but we soon grew weary of our travel schedules and hated being apart so often. So, we committed to doing something brave and daring, something that would allow us to be our own bosses and give us the freedom to hang out with one another whenever we wanted. It had always been a quiet little dream of mine to one day open a bakery, and when I began caring more about the cookies I was serving at my staff meetings than the topics on the agenda, I went to Kev with my idea of opening a vegan bakery. To my delight, he was into it! Later, when we began brainstorming names for our new business, we were standing in Kevin's office, rattling off all sorts of ideas and making scrunched-up faces at one another while firmly shaking our heads. I suspect it was something akin to expectant moms and dads trying to come up with baby names. Exasperated, Kevin sighed "Bunner," and both of our faces lit up. We had a name for our dream.

At first I couldn't see how any of the foods I loved would fit into my new lifestyle without dairy or eggs, baking cakes and cookies seemed impossible. But as the weeks passed, I began to adjust, and my love of food meant I was unwilling to just give up on the things I loved to eat.

Within the year I had left my job and took to the kitchen like a woman on a mission. Although I'd kept baking since becoming vegan, I had been craving the treats from my childhood that I hadn't been able to find anywhere: butter tarts, birthday cake, donuts, waffles, pancakes, scones. I knew that I couldn't be the only vegan who loved the choice she had made but didn't want to have to leave moist, chocolaty brownies in the past. In the meantime, I had also become intrigued with the gluten-free diet, and basically all allergies; I suspected that if it was a bummer for me to give up my favourite things willingly, it must be horrible to have to give them up unwillingly.

So I started experimenting with vegan, gluten-free takes on the comfort foods Kev and I loved. I got my feet wet with a few simple recipes, for cupcakes and cookies, but soon realized that gluten-free baking was going to be just as challenging, if not more, than vegan baking had been. I was using all sorts of flours I wasn't familiar with, and had to teach myself through trial and error how each flour and starch differed in texture and taste, not to mention how they went with one another when blended.

While I was recipe-testing, Kevin was taste-testing. After every new baked good came out of the oven, I would get him to critique if for me. Sounds like a dream job, right? Well, having a manufacturing background, in which quality control was king, Kev took this role very seriously, and anyone who knows me knows that this could also be a potentially dangerous job (insert "You think my cookies need *what*?" here). That said, what Kev brought to the table was priceless. Not only did he often make the products better, but he really encouraged us to work as a team, which in turn made our business stronger. Even today, Kev is still tinkering with tried-and-true recipes and processes, giving them what we call "the Mackie touch," and sure enough, his constant striving for improvement seems to better whatever he has his sights set on.

As the fall of 2010 swirled in and the farmers' market where we sold our goodies closed down for the season, I continued to receive a flurry of phone calls (and the $800 cell-phone bill to prove it) from people who couldn't bear to give up our treats for the winter. It was shocking to us, but we were the city's only vegan bakery *and* the city's only gluten-free bakery. We had found a very heavily populated and untapped niche! Without a storefront to sell from, I took to the streets on my bike and spent a few months delivering muffins and cookies around the city, to the great excitement of my previously deprived customers. Before long I was getting requests for birthday cakes, so back to the kitchen I went, teaching myself how to make vegan, gluten-free cakes, and then how to frost them so that they looked as beautiful as they tasted.

> When I began caring more about the cookies I was serving at my staff meetings than the topics on the agenda, I went to Kev with my idea of opening a vegan bakery.

By the end of that fall, it was clear that there was too much demand to keep filling orders from my kitchen. Kevin and I were feeling a bit overwhelmed, but we didn't have enough capital to rent a bakery space near our apartment in downtown Toronto. Exhausted after a night of fruitless brainstorming on what to do next, we went out for brunch in a west-end neighbourhood called the Junction. As we wandered around to burn off the scrambled tofu, Kevin spotted a tiny handwritten For Rent sign in a shop across the street. We took a look through the window and were surprised to see the landlady inside waving us in. It took only about 10 minutes of investigating the small but perfectly appointed space for us to decide it simply had to be Bunner's. We dazzled the landlady with our charm and the next day signed the lease and gave her our first and last months' rent. We opened our doors about two weeks later, and the rest is Bunner's history!

We've never advertised but have instead relied on word of mouth from happy vegan and gluten-free customers who rave about our French Toast Cupcake or Glazed Chocolate Donut to other friends who have been craving the same kinds of comfort foods Kev and I were dreaming of just a few years ago.

Since that day in fall 2010, we have been lucky to attract a crowd of amazing, loyal, and fun-loving customers whose mass grows daily. We've never advertised but have instead relied on word of mouth from happy vegan and gluten-free customers who rave about our French Toast Cupcake or Glazed Chocolate Donut to other friends who have been craving the same kinds of comfort foods Kev and I were dreaming of just a few years ago. Together with our team and our band of loyal customers, we've created a little monster that we are so proud of.

When Kevin and I were approached to do this cookbook, we were a little anxious about the work that would go into it (and rightfully so!), but it seemed like the right time to reach out beyond the boundaries of our neighbourhood bakery. Now we finally have a response for customers who want pumpkin pie in July (turn to page 195) or people in Victoria who have heard about our birthday cake and are wondering if we can ship across the country (no, but turn to page 129 for the recipe). It's been so energizing and exciting to share our tips and secret recipes so that our vegan, gluten-free treats can be available whenever and wherever our loving friends want them.

I developed many of these recipes in my home kitchen before Bunner's was even around, so I know they're going to be as straightforward for you to make as they were for me. We may make 200 chocolate chip cookies now instead of 24, but the recipes and methods are the same. We all take so much pride in each and every little morsel that makes its way to you because Kevin and I, and all our amazing staff, truly love what we do and what we're making.

So with that, roll up your sleeves, get the Van Halen pumping, and have a great time! You might stumble a bit if you're completely new to baking, but have faith and you will turn out beautiful and delicious treats.

PANTRY PRIMER

We are all born either a cook or a baker. Cooks are a flamboyant bunch in the kitchen and often cook with unfettered abandon, dashing spices every which way. Bakers are more steadfast, love to follow recipes to the letter, and are usually more reserved in their experimentations. If you're a baker, terrific!—you'll be right at home. Go on, now, and bake up some delicious cookies. If, however, you are more of a cook, please take the following advice to heart:

- Be sure to read the recipe through before you start. If you're having a dinner party in a few hours, you won't be a happy camper when you get to the last line of an involved recipe only to realize that the dessert actually needs to firm up overnight.

- Measure things correctly and with the proper tools. A "teaspoon"—of baking soda, say—is an exact measurement, not a guideline, not a pinch, not the small spoon in the cutlery drawer that you use to stir your tea.

- Don't open the oven, even once, to look at your treats before the baking time is up. Poking and prodding your little creations before they're at least three-quarters of the way through baking can be disastrous, especially with delicate things like cakes. Instead, turn on the oven light and peek through the window.

- The raw batters will probably taste weird, but don't be alarmed. If you're used to taste-testing batters, you should plan to skip that step, especially with the cupcakes. I don't know what sort of strange gluten-free alchemy is at work, but some batters just taste awful. Post-baking, they taste like perfection!

With that out of the way, let's have some fun! Here is a description of every tip, tool, and ingredient you'll need to master the recipes in this book.

Tools

···

Airtight containers: Perfect for storing your goodies in if you plan to enjoy them over several days. Most of the treats in this book are best stored in these containers at room temperature.

Baking equipment: If you don't already have a variety that you've inherited or bought over the years, I suggest getting two baking sheets, a 9-inch glass pie plate, two 9-inch metal cake pans, a 9-inch square metal pan, and two 12-cup muffin pans (some of the cupcake recipes make 18 cupcakes, so you'll need to prepare one and a half muffin pans).

Bowls: You'll need at least one set of three nesting bowls in sizes small, medium, and large.

Canola spray: A godsend when you're baking cakes or squares, canola spray ensures that they don't stick to the baking pans. At the bakery, we use the Spectrum brand of canola spray, which is made from organic canola that has not been genetically engineered and contains zero hexane or chemical preservatives.

Cooling rack: This is a wire mesh rack that stands about ½ inch off the countertop. It allows air to freely circulate around items in hot pans or de-panned items, cooling them evenly and quickly on all sides. If you place a hot pan directly on an insulating surface like a countertop, the item in it will keep baking thanks to the residual heat of the pan. If a hot de-panned baked good is placed directly on an insulating surface, its released steam will condense underneath it and turn the edges soft or soggy.

Double boiler: Sometimes referred to as a *bain-marie*, which is a bit more romantic-sounding, a double boiler is typically used for gentle heating, as when melting chocolate, which burns easily. You can buy a double boiler for this purpose, or you can do what we do: Pour 1 or 2 inches of water into a medium pot, and place a small heatproof bowl in the water. Place the chocolate in the bowl, being careful not to splash any water into it (or it will seize up). Melt over medium heat, keeping a watchful eye and stirring occasionally. *Voilà!* Beautifully melted chocolate.

Food processor: This tool is definitely worth the investment. With it you can whip up the dough for pastries, scones, biscuits, and more in a jiffy. On your non-baking days, use it to prep veggies and even make smoothies.

What Is Veganism?

Veganism is the elimination of all animal- or insect-derived ingredients from one's diet. So, broadly, vegans don't eat meat, fish, dairy, eggs, or honey. The reasons for becoming vegan vary from person to person, though many people adopt a vegan lifestyle for health reasons, ethical reasons, or because of its positive environmental impact. Or for all three. A vegan diet is 100% free of cholesterol and is insanely heart-healthy. It's also been proven to reverse diabetes and is just a great way to boost your energy, feel lighter, and get glowing!

Veganism can seem extreme to some, but Kev and I believe there's nothing excessive about wanting to be compassionate and to express that compassion in your lifestyle.

What Is Gluten-Free?

A gluten-free diet is one that excludes gluten. Gluten (the Latin word for glue) is a protein in wheat products that acts very much like a glue by giving texture and stretch to products such as bread and pizza dough. For some people with gluten sensitivities, it can cause adverse reactions ranging from mild skin rashes to severe stomach discomfort. For those with celiac disease, eating wheat can cause intense inflammation in the intestine. At the bakery I've met countless people who were sick their entire lives—that is, before they adopted gluten-free diets and began to feel so much better.

There are many possible symptoms of gluten allergies. If you suspect you are gluten-sensitive or have celiac disease, try cutting wheat from your diet for a few weeks to see how you feel, or talk to a health-care professional who has experience with this allergy.

Measuring cups and spoons: For the recipes in this book, I've used nesting measuring cups (the type that stack inside one another) rather than the big glass pouring-style measuring cups with a spout. Believe it or not, volumes can vary widely between the two types, so for the best results, use nesting cups, even for the liquids. My favourites are basic stainless-steel cup-and-spoon sets. I do also have a pouring-style measuring cup, though, to help out with liquids and sauces.

Oven thermometer: You've probably heard it a hundred times, but I'll say it again: everyone's oven is different. Your oven might run hotter or cooler than what the dial or display suggests, and the result could be over- or undercooked treats. Use a high-temperature oven thermometer to adjust your cooking temperatures.

Parchment paper: This is a must when baking items on a baking sheet. This magic paper is both water and grease resistant, eliminates the need to grease the pans (making cleanup a cinch), and practically guarantees your prized batch of cookies won't stick or melt onto the hot baking sheet (in fact, they'll slide right off). As an added bonus, you can pick up the whole batch of piping-hot goodies and easily transfer them to a cooling rack without fumbling with spatulas and hot pans.

Rolling pin: Any rolling pin will do, but you absolutely need one if you plan on making any of our pastries or pies, the cinnamon rolls or rugelach.

Sifter: Use this to sift powdered sugar and flours—no one likes to bite into a clump of flour in their muffin, or crunch into a granular cupcake frosting. At the bakery we exclusively use a double-mesh sifter, which has, as the name suggests, not one but two layers of mesh. This helps achieve the finest separation of powdered sugar and other dry ingredients.

Spatula: Any spatula will do as long as the blade is stiff enough to scrape the bottom of the bowl containing your batters, catching any wayward unmixed flour.

Springform pan: This tool is a must if you plan on making the cheesecake recipes in this book. It's the shape of a regular 8-inch cake pan but with removable sides so you don't have to disturb your creamy delight when it comes time to serve it.

Stand and hand mixers: The stand mixer at Bunner's makes many of the regular tasks in a bakery so much easier than they might otherwise be. That said, I know it's a large purchase and may be appropriate only for the most committed, diehard bakers of the bunch. In this case you'll want to invest in a little hand mixer, which you will be grateful for when it comes time to make frosting. If you're living off the grid and totally dedicated to baking the way your grandma's grandma did, you can use a potato masher to cream up the fats for things like frostings and shortbread cookies. I've done this on a couple of occasions with pretty good results.

Whisk: Be sure to get one with a nice substantial feel, one that will stand up to those headstrong cupcake batters. For strength, metal wire is best.

Other bits and bobs: If you're a real keener, you'll be interested in getting a few other pieces of equipment, especially if you plan to make donuts or waffles. These include a pastry brush (to wash pie crusts with non-dairy milk, for instance), citrus zester, frosting spatula (for the smoothest spread), waffle iron, donut pans, ice-cream scoop (commercial bakeries buy these in different sizes for consistent portioning of everything from cookie dough to cupcake batter), and, if you love them, novelty-shaped cookie cutters and cake pans.

Ingredients

It's so, so important to use the highest-quality ingredients you can find. No matter how tasty-sounding the recipe is, combining low-quality ingredients with more low-quality ingredients will only result in one thing: low-quality treats. Of course, you'll have to use whatever is available to you; just make sure it's the highest quality you can find. I encourage you to search out ingredients that are organic and fairly traded, and especially to look for produce that's in season and locally grown, and sold at your local farmers' market. I know that "organic," "fair trade," and "local" are often shrugged off as being just buzzwords, but I feel these qualities truly do make a difference. An apple that has to travel for days to get to us, and that has been sprayed with countless pesticides and ripening agents, is just not going to taste as fresh and delicious as the one from the organic farm an hour down the road.

FLOURS

Bob's Red Mill garbanzo and fava flour: This flour is terrific in gluten-free baking. The texture it produces is fluffy and so lends itself perfectly to cupcakes. Some people worry about a beany taste, but when properly combined with the right ingredients, the result is a light bite of heaven. As an added bonus for our vegan friends, garbanzo and fava flour provides a protein boost while minimizing the carbs.

Bob's Red Mill gluten-free all-purpose flour: I love this stuff! It takes so much of the guesswork out of our recipes. The key to any gluten-free baking is successfully combining the different flours and starches, and this gluten-free, all-purpose flour is a great blend of garbanzo bean flour, fava bean flour, tapioca flour, sorghum flour, and potato starch. It also makes things less complicated in that you need only invest in one flour. Just a word of caution, though: Don't use this to substitute the flour in recipes that don't call for it. I promise, if it worked, we would mention it.

Brown rice flour: This is the flour people most commonly associate with gluten-free baking. Rice flour too is terrific in some recipes, but because it creates a fairly dense and sometimes grainy texture, it's best for cookies and pastries—though we do also use it in some of our cakes to give them a bit of structure.

STARCHES & OTHER THICKENERS

Agar-agar: This is a vegetable-based gelatin made of a variety of seaweeds. It can come in powder or flake form, and when boiled with a liquid, can do wonders for thickening up your desserts. We use it in our pumpkin pie (page 195), and the results are a perfectly creamy, dreamy pie filling.

Arrowroot starch: This light starch can be used in baking and for thickening. In baking, we use it in conjunction with other gluten-free flours and starches to create a soft and light crumb. It also makes a fantastic thickener for our lemon curd and caramel sauce. Unlike cornstarch, arrowroot starch does not cloud a mixture but dissolves clear, making it perfect for fruit sauces and glazes.

Potato starch: In baking, starches are all about texture. Gluten-free and alternative flours have a reputation for being dense or having a weird texture; the key is to blend the flour with starch. Potato starch is my preference, as it helps retain structure while creating a delicate and light crumb in cakes and the like.

Xanthan gum: Xanthan gum has incredible thickening and binding properties, and so is a great aid in gluten-free baking. By adding a little to a gluten-free flour mix, you can nearly replicate some of the thickness and structural characteristics of gluten that help hold the baked good together. Without xanthan gum, all we'd be holding is a pile of crumbs! A little goes a long way, so a small amount will last you for a while.

FATS

Canola oil: Canola oil is a great delicate-tasting oil to use in baked goods. We use Spectrum, which is an organic, non-GMO canola brand. Be sure not to use the first-pressed oils (it will be labelled on the bottle) in these recipes, as they have an intense taste that is definitely not suitable for baking. If you want to substitute, grapeseed oil is an excellent choice.

Coconut oil: This is a nice shortening-like option that helps you achieve that sought-after buttery taste. Be sure to look for refined coconut oil, which doesn't have a strong coconut taste. Solid at room temperature, coconut oil needs to be melted before use in recipes. Melt it on the stovetop over low heat, or leave out on the countertop if the temperature in your home is 24°C (75°F) or higher. We use Omega Nutrition brand, but there are many other brands of quality coconut oil on the market too.

Non-hydrogenated vegan butter and shortening: We use the products of a company called Earth Balance, which to date is the only one out there making vegan butter and shortening. For baking we always use the vegan "buttery" sticks, which have handy tablespoon marks on the packaging to guide you in measuring accurately and cutting off however much you need. You can use the tubs of buttery spread instead if you're in a jam, or substitute the soy-free buttery spread if you are avoiding soy products. If you do substitute, the resulting product may be a bit softer, especially for something like frosting or pastry, and should have some extra time in the refrigerator to firm up.

EGG SUBSTITUTES

Applesauce: Applesauce is a nice replacement for eggs in baked goods. The applesauce we use in the recipes is unsweetened and without cinnamon or any other spice. A general rule of thumb is ¼ cup applesauce for every egg you'd like to replace (up to two eggs). This keeps your baking moist, and the bonus is that you'll be keeping cholesterol levels down.

Coconut yogurt: This is a favourite of mine for snacking, but it's also helpful in baking to replace eggs. It gives that richness back to baked goods where eggs have been removed and keeps your goodies from getting dry.

Naming Names

You'll see that in many places we suggest using specific brands of ingredients. We don't want you to think we're just shilling you some brand loyalty. No, the fact of the matter is that we've tried everything, and these products work in these specific recipes—they are tried, tested, and true! Vegan and gluten-free products are often not single, refined, or processed ingredients, as milk or wheat flour are, and so they can vary quite widely in their composition. One vegan cream cheese may be created with an entirely different set of ingredients from another. And so we name names here. We'd hate to see you spend your hard-earned money on ingredients that just aren't going to work in our recipes. So, if you see us calling a brand out, we've done so intentionally. Heed our advice and you will turn out the perfectly baked little scrumptious morsels of your dreams.

NON-DAIRY MILKS

There are three types of unsweetened non-dairy milks we suggest using for the recipes in this book. If it's not specified in the ingredients list, feel free to use your choice of the following:

Coconut milk: The full-fat canned version is akin to heavy cream and comes in a can. We use it to add body and flavour to butter tarts, frostings, and cinnamon buns.

Rice milk: This is quite thin but great for adding an extra splash of moisture to batters. Do not, however, use it for those recipes calling for a milk to be soured with vinegar to make "buttermilk"—here, a creamier milk like soy or coconut from the carton is needed.

Soy or coconut milk beverage: These are a bit more creamy and good for making buttermilk. Coconut milk beverage is the one you buy in a carton, not a can. The thicker and richer soy creamer is also excellent in frostings or any recipe where coconut milk is called for.

A note on almond milk: We don't use nuts in the bakery, so it's not an ingredient we've tested in these recipes, but if it's your preferred milk alternative, give it a try.

SWEETENERS

Agave nectar: We use agave nectar as a sweetener in our cakes and cupcakes because it provides an extra bit of moisture and a delicate sweetness that differs from that of organic sugar. The type we use is the raw agave from Madhava, which is sustainably grown and completely organic.

Organic powdered sugar: Wholesome Sweeteners makes the only organic and unrefined powdered sugar that I know of. It's simply pulverized organic sugar mixed with a tiny bit of starch so that it doesn't clump. You will definitely need to sift this sugar before using it because it's not as powdery fine as a commercial refined icing sugar. At the bakery, we hand-sift it through a double-mesh sifter to ensure the finest powder possible.

Organic sugar: Also known as evaporated cane juice, this sweetener is naturally rich in minerals and vitamins and is the result when the juice is extracted from the sugar cane and left to evaporate, forming sweet little crystals. Refined white sugar has been bleached and stripped of all nutritional value, so please use high-quality organic sugar, which is kinder to your body. The brand we prefer is Wholesome Sweeteners, an organic and fair-trade company.

Sucanat: Sucanat is a raw brown sugar. Because it is unrefined and retains its nutrient-rich molasses, Sucanat is terrific for things that require an extra bit of richness, like brownies and butter tarts. Compared with a lower-quality refined and processed brown sugar, Sucanat has a smaller proportion of sucrose and is loaded with vitamins and minerals, including potassium, calcium, magnesium, and vitamin A. Again, we use Wholesome Sweeteners brand.

CHOCOLATE

Unsweetened cocoa powder: Using quality cocoa powder in baking is crucial to the product's outcome. I've used various cocoas over the years, but my absolute favourite is Cocoa Camino, which is completely organic and fair trade. Some of the best chocolatiers and bakeries in Toronto use this cocoa too, so you'll be swinging with the best of them.

Vegan chocolate chips: It's a common belief that all chocolate has milk in it, but chocolate comes from cacao beans, which, when last I checked, don't contain dairy. The brand we use is Enjoy Life—these chips are allergen-free (and so small and cute!). I also recommend Cocoa Camino semi-sweet (55% cocoa) chocolate chips, made from organic and fair-trade chocolate.

FLAVOURINGS

Flavour extracts: These can be so much fun to play around with in the kitchen. Add a few drops to vanilla buttercream to come up with a whole new flavour! My favourites are mint, lemon, and orange. You can also find maple and rum extracts in specialty stores. Many extracts contain wheat alcohol, so check with the manufacturer if gluten is a top concern. Alternately, use an oil-based flavour like Frontier or Simply Organic.

Vanilla extract: This is another one of those crucial ingredients that can make or break your goodies. I always invest in a high-quality vanilla for great flavour and aromatic qualities. After all your hard work, you want your goodies to be the best! Frontier makes really good vanilla, as does Nielsen-Massey, which is what we use at the bakery.

EXTRA GOODIES

Daiya cheese shreds: Daiya is the only vegan cheese I've found that I like. It comes shredded and in blocks, and the company releases new vegan "cheese" innovations all the time. We use the shreds in the recipes here to help give the savoury dishes a bit of that salty, melty cheesiness.

Gluten-free bread crumbs: If you can't find these at the grocery store, don't fret: they're a breeze to make. Using the gluten-free bread of your choice (or crackers, cornflakes, or even corn tortilla chips), buzz up as much as you think you'll need in a food processor, until they're broken down into fine crumbs.

Gluten-free oats: Oats can be a contentious issue in the gluten-free world. We get our oats from Bob's Red Mill, which tests every batch for gluten contamination and packages only the pure gluten-free oats, in its own facility. Actually, the oats themselves are not the issue; it's that they are often processed in facilities that process wheat, leading to cross-contamination. A very small percentage of the population cannot tolerate even pure gluten-free oats; if you're part of that percentage, you may want to steer clear of the recipes that use oats.

Silken tofu: We don't use too much tofu at the bakery, since we like to keep things as soy-free as possible, but this one definitely needs explanation. There is firm tofu, which is often used in savoury dishes, cubed, and then there is silken tofu, which is very soft and used in desserts and dressings. Silken tofu is often packaged in shelf-stable, non-refrigerated containers and available at supermarkets and health food stores. To further complicate things, the silken tofu called for may be either soft or firm, depending on what it's being used for. We use both styles in this cookbook but always specify which one to use.

MEASUREMENT EQUIVALENTS

These measurement equivalents will help you double or halve any of the recipes in this book:

1 tablespoon = 3 teaspoons
¼ cup = 4 tablespoons
⅓ cup = 5 tablespoons
½ cup = 8 tablespoons
⅔ cup = 10 tablespoons
¾ cup = 12 tablespoons
1 cup = 16 tablespoons

BREAKFAST OF CHAMPIONS

As a baker, I rise and eat earlier than most people would find decent, and generally waffles and cinnamon buns are not on the agenda. Workday mornings usually consist of a green smoothie or a quick bowl of oatmeal before I hop on my motorcycle and zoom off to work. But on those days I have to myself, you'll find me doing pirouettes in the kitchen while I happily whip up a tall stack of pancakes or a tasty plate of scones to go with my tea. So, good morning, sweethearts! It's time to fuel up with some beautiful breakfasts.

Sunday Morning Cornmeal Waffles 25

Buttermilk Pancakes 27

Supersonic Granola 29

Banana Date Scones 31

Lemon Blackberry Scones 33

Amelia's "Seal the Deal" Pumpkin Scones 35

Cinnamon Buns 39

SUNDAY MORNING CORNMEAL WAFFLES

Makes 5 large Belgian-style waffles

Admittedly, when I'm out and about, I prefer a savoury brunch. That said, homemade waffles slay me. If you don't have a waffle iron at home, you should get one! You may use it only a couple of times a year, but it's so worth it. The other beauty about waffles is that they're simple to make—Kev and I once manned the breakfast tent on a camping expedition and managed to keep our weary gang's spirits high with these quick and easy waffles.

This recipe is all about texture—the cornmeal produces a crunchy outside, and the buttermilk makes them light and fluffy on the inside. I love to pair these with homemade lemon curd (page 243) and fresh blueberries, or an organic blueberry sauce.

1¾ cups soy or coconut milk beverage	½ teaspoon xanthan gum
1 tablespoon apple cider vinegar	½ teaspoon sea salt
1 cup Bob's Red Mill gluten-free all-purpose flour	¼ cup unsweetened applesauce
1 cup cornmeal	¼ cup canola oil
1 tablespoon organic sugar	½ teaspoon vanilla extract
2 teaspoons gluten-free baking powder	½ teaspoon lemon extract
½ teaspoon baking soda	

Preheat the waffle iron. In a small bowl, combine the milk and vinegar. The reaction of these two ingredients raises the acidity of the milk and causes it to thicken somewhat. Set aside for at least 10 minutes to allow the milk to become "buttermilk."

In a large bowl, sift the flour and add the cornmeal, sugar, baking powder, baking soda, xanthan gum, and salt. In a small bowl, whisk together the applesauce, oil, and vanilla and lemon extracts. Add the wet ingredients to the dry ingredients, then add the buttermilk. Mix to combine.

Spray the waffle iron with canola spray. Depending on the size of your waffle iron, pour a scant ¼ cup batter for classic waffle makers and ⅓ cup batter for Belgian waffle makers onto the griddle. Close the lid and cook for 4 to 5 minutes before opening the lid to check doneness. The waffles will be a golden brown, with a crispy surface, when they're ready. Remove from the griddle.

Repeat until all the batter is used. Serve with vegan butter and dark maple syrup. For some next-level breakfasting, add a dollop of coconut whipped cream (page 245).

TIP: If you have any leftover coconut bacon from The Lumberjack (page 123), throw a handful on top of the waffle batter before closing the lid on the waffle iron.

BUTTERMILK PANCAKES

Makes 6 silver-dollar pancakes

I went through a phase where every weekend I had to make pancakes. Obsessed, I would rifle through my cupboards to see what kind of flavour concoction I could make that week. The nice thing about this pancake recipe is that it's adaptable, as you will see in the variations given below. You can throw almost anything in and it will turn out amazing, so don't be afraid to get creative. This recipe makes enough for two people, but you can easily double or triple it to serve more.

1 cup soy or coconut milk beverage	1 teaspoon gluten-free baking powder
1 tablespoon apple cider vinegar	¼ teaspoon baking soda
½ cup potato starch	¼ teaspoon xanthan gum
½ cup Bob's Red Mill garbanzo and fava flour	¼ teaspoon sea salt
	¼ cup unsweetened applesauce
3 tablespoons tapioca starch	2 tablespoons canola oil
1 tablespoon organic sugar	1 teaspoon vanilla extract

In a small bowl, combine the milk and vinegar. The reaction of these two ingredients raises the acidity of the milk and causes it to thicken somewhat. Set aside for at least 10 minutes to allow the milk to become "buttermilk."

In a large bowl, sift together the potato starch, flour, tapioca starch, sugar, baking powder, baking soda, xanthan gum, and salt. Whisk to combine. In a small bowl, whisk together the applesauce, oil, and vanilla. Add the wet ingredients to the dry ingredients, then pour in the buttermilk. Whisk to combine. If adding any other ingredients (chocolate chips, berries, nuts), fold them in now. Let the batter sit for about 10 minutes to thicken and become puffy.

Heat a large frying pan over medium-high heat. Coat the pan with canola spray or coconut oil. Once the pan is hot, pour in batter to desired pancake size—I find that about ¼ cup per pancake is a good size—fitting as many in the pan at one time as possible. Cook for 3 to 5 minutes, until bubbles form on the top, then use a spatula to flip. Cook for another 2 to 4 minutes. Don't press the pancakes down with the spatula while they're cooking, as this will make them dense, not fluffy.

Enjoy with a pat of vegan butter or coconut butter and a generous drizzle of dark maple syrup.

VARIATIONS

Peanut Butter and Chocolate-Chip Pancakes: Add 1 cup vegan semi-sweet chocolate chips before letting the batter sit. Spread pancakes generously with your favourite peanut butter before gobbling them up.

Banana Walnut Pancakes: Replace the applesauce with ¼ cup mashed ripe banana. Mix in ¾ cup walnuts before letting batter sit.

SUPERSONIC GRANOLA

Makes about 8 cups

Supersonic granola was one of our earliest creations, hailing from the days when we sold our goodies at the farmers' market under a 10- × 10-foot canopy. Back in those days we had a customer named Richard, who was crazy about this granola. He even had us regularly deliver it to his office (our only delivery customer at the time, he had me pedalling across Toronto to get there!).

Homemade granola is exceedingly simple to make; use this recipe as a guide to making your own concoctions, if you like. If you're feeling inspired, swap out the seeds for your favourite nuts, or use maple syrup instead of agave nectar—the world of granola-making is now in your hands!

4 cups gluten-free oats

2 tablespoons ground cinnamon

½ teaspoon sea salt

¾ cup raw, unsalted pumpkin seeds

¾ cup raw, unsalted sunflower seeds

½ cup whole flaxseed

½ cup unsweetened shredded coconut

⅔ cup agave nectar

⅓ cup melted coconut oil

1 cup dried cranberries

Preheat the oven to 300°F and line two baking sheets with parchment paper.

In a large bowl, mix together the oats, cinnamon, and salt. Add the pumpkin and sunflower seeds, flaxseed, and coconut and mix well. Add the agave nectar and oil and toss until everything is evenly coated.

Split the mixture evenly between the two pans, spreading it in a single layer. Bake for 15 minutes, then gently push around the mixture in the pans with a wooden spoon. Bake for another 15 minutes.

Initially, the granola won't feel crunchy—this happens as it cools. Let the granola cool until it's easily handled, then transfer to the large bowl. Once completely cool, add the dried cranberries and use your hands to break up the granola. Store in an airtight container for up to 2 weeks.

VARIATION

Chocolate Chip Granola: Add 1 cup vegan semi-sweet chocolate chips along with the cranberries.

BANANA DATE SCONES

Makes 8 scones

Banana is one of my favourite baking ingredients. Its moisture and binding properties allow you to eliminate the eggs in a recipe, and the aroma is amazing. But keep in mind that banana influences the taste of the mixture it's added to, often resulting in "Banana [fill in name of your treat here]."

The chopped dates in these scones provide a flavourful and vibrant surprise to bite into. Not overly sweet, these make a great addition to picnic baskets and a lovely mid-afternoon treat.

3 tablespoons soy or coconut milk beverage

¼ teaspoon apple cider vinegar

1 cup Bob's Red Mill garbanzo and fava flour

½ cup brown rice flour

½ cup potato starch

2 tablespoons organic sugar

1 tablespoon + ¼ teaspoon gluten-free baking powder

2 teaspoons ground cinnamon

½ teaspoon xanthan gum

½ teaspoon sea salt

7 tablespoons Earth Balance Buttery Sticks, chilled

¾ cup mashed ripe banana (1½ to 2 freckled bananas)

3 tablespoons dark maple syrup

1 cup coarsely chopped pitted dates

1 batch donut glaze (page 237) (optional)

Preheat the oven to 350°F. Line a baking sheet with parchment paper.

In a small bowl, combine the milk and vinegar. The reaction of these two ingredients raises the acidity of the milk and causes it to thicken somewhat. Set aside for at least 10 minutes to allow the milk to become "buttermilk."

In a large bowl, sift both flours with the potato starch, sugar, baking powder, cinnamon, xanthan gum, and salt. Transfer to a food processor and pulse a few times to blend. Add the butter in tablespoon-size chunks and pulse until the mixture takes on a sandy consistency.

In a medium bowl, whisk together the banana and maple syrup. Add to the dry ingredients in the food processor, along with the buttermilk. Pulse a few times until the dough comes together, scraping down the sides of the processor as necessary. Transfer the dough to a large bowl and fold in the dates.

If you prefer triangular scones, turn out the dough onto a well-floured surface, patting it into a disc-like shape about 1¼ inches thick. Cut as you would a pie, into eight triangle shapes. Using a flat spatula, transfer the triangles to the prepared baking sheet. If you prefer round scones, measure the dough out into ⅓-cup portions and loosely hand-form into eight balls. Place on the prepared baking sheet.

Bake for about 15 minutes, until the scones develop the slightest hint of a tan on top and the bottoms are a light golden colour. Remove pan from the oven and transfer scones to a cooling rack.

Serve as is or drizzled with donut glaze.

LEMON BLACKBERRY SCONES

Makes 8 scones

Lemon and blackberry make a terrific pairing in this scone, which has a delicate and tender crumb thanks to the applesauce. As with all the scone recipes in this book, this recipe calls for a food processor; however, if you're particularly good at improvising, you could get away with using a pastry blender or slicing the butter into the dough with a couple of flat-bladed knives. These scones should be served within the first couple days of making them, to fully appreciate their lovely texture.

3 tablespoons soy or coconut milk beverage

¼ teaspoon apple cider vinegar

1 cup Bob's Red Mill garbanzo and fava flour

½ cup brown rice flour

½ cup potato starch

¼ cup organic sugar

1 tablespoon gluten-free baking powder

½ teaspoon xanthan gum

½ teaspoon sea salt

7 tablespoons Earth Balance Buttery Sticks, chilled

¾ cup unsweetened applesauce

3 tablespoons agave nectar

1½ teaspoons lemon extract

1 cup fresh or frozen blackberries

Glaze

½ cup + 2 tablespoons powdered sugar

1 tablespoon agave nectar

1 tablespoon non-dairy milk

½ teaspoon lemon extract

Zest of 1 lemon (optional)

Preheat the oven to 350°F. Line a baking sheet with parchment paper.

In a small bowl, combine the milk and vinegar. The reaction of these two ingredients raises the acidity of the milk and causes it to thicken somewhat. Set aside for at least 10 minutes to allow the milk to become "buttermilk."

In a medium bowl, sift both flours with the potato starch, sugar, baking powder, xanthan gum, and salt. Transfer to a food processor and pulse a few times to blend. Add the butter in tablespoon-size chunks and pulse until the mixture takes on a sandy consistency.

In a medium bowl, whisk together the applesauce, agave nectar, and lemon extract. Add to the dry ingredients in the food processor, along with the buttermilk. Pulse a few times until the dough comes together, scraping down the sides of the processor as necessary. Transfer to a large bowl and gently fold in the blackberries.

If you prefer triangular scones, turn out the dough onto a well-floured surface, patting it into a disc-like shape about 1¼ inches thick. Cut as you would a pie, into eight triangle shapes. Using a flat spatula, transfer the triangles to the prepared baking sheet. *(continued on page 34)*

If you prefer round scones, measure the dough out into ⅓-cup portions and loosely hand-form into eight balls. Place on the prepared baking sheet.

Bake for about 15 minutes, until the scones develop the slightest hint of a tan on top and the bottoms are a light golden colour. Remove from the oven and transfer scones to a cooling rack.

While the scones are cooling, prepare the glaze.

For the glaze: Sift the powdered sugar into a small bowl, then whisk in the agave nectar, non-dairy milk, lemon extract, and lemon zest (if using) until smooth.

Use a fork or spoon to decoratively drizzle the glaze in a zigzag pattern over each scone, or simply dip the top of each scone directly into the glaze. Let the glaze harden slightly before serving.

AMELIA'S "SEAL THE DEAL" PUMPKIN SCONES

Makes 8 scones

This perfect little scone is the brainchild of Amelia Earl, one of our all-star bakers and manager of our Junction shop. While we were interviewing for a new baker's position, Amelia strolled into the bakery with a box of these homemade beauties and won us over instantly.

With just the perfect amount of scone-y density, and a generous drizzle of maple glaze, these scones will satisfy your sweet tooth without going overboard. They're perfect alongside your favourite tea, especially on those cooler fall mornings. As a bonus, pumpkin is both an antioxidant and a great source of vitamin A, so I guess what I'm saying is, they're like a vitamin! Just kidding, sweethearts, let's not get carried away.

3 tablespoons soy or coconut milk beverage

¼ teaspoon apple cider vinegar

1 cup Bob's Red Mill garbanzo and fava flour

½ cup brown rice flour

½ cup potato starch

¼ cup organic sugar

1 tablespoon + ¼ teaspoon gluten-free baking powder

½ teaspoon xanthan gum

½ teaspoon sea salt

½ teaspoon ground cinnamon

¼ teaspoon ground nutmeg

7 tablespoons Earth Balance Buttery Sticks, chilled

¾ cup pure pumpkin purée

3 tablespoons maple syrup

Maple Nutmeg Glaze

1⅓ cups organic powdered sugar

2 tablespoons maple syrup

1 tablespoon non-dairy milk

½ teaspoon vanilla extract

Pinch ground nutmeg

Preheat the oven to 350°F. Line a baking sheet with parchment paper.

In a small bowl, combine the milk and vinegar. The reaction of these two ingredients raises the acidity of the milk and causes it to thicken somewhat. Set aside for at least 10 minutes to allow the milk to become "buttermilk."

In a medium bowl, sift both flours with the potato starch, sugar, baking powder, xanthan gum, salt, cinnamon, and nutmeg. Transfer to a food processor and pulse a few times to blend. Add the butter in tablespoon-size chunks and pulse until the mixture takes on a sandy consistency.

In a medium bowl, whisk together the pumpkin purée and maple syrup. Add to the dry ingredients in the food processor, along with the buttermilk. Pulse a few times until the dough comes together, scraping down the sides of the processor as necessary.

(continued on page 36)

If you prefer triangular scones, turn out the dough onto a well-floured surface, patting it into a disc-like shape about 1¼ inches thick. Cut as you would a pie, into eight triangle shapes. Using a flat spatula, transfer the triangles to the prepared baking sheet.

If you prefer round scones, measure the dough out into ⅓-cup portions and loosely hand-form into eight balls. Place on the prepared baking sheet.

Bake for about 15 minutes, until the scones develop the slightest hint of a tan on top and the bottoms are a light golden colour. Remove from the oven and transfer scones to a cooling rack.

While the scones are cooling, prepare the glaze.

For the glaze: In a medium bowl, sift the sugar, then add the maple syrup, non-dairy milk, and vanilla. Using a fork, whisk the ingredients together until you achieve a thick icing. Stir in the nutmeg.

Use a fork or spoon to decoratively drizzle the glaze in a zigzag pattern over each scone, or simply dip the top of each scone directly into the glaze. If you are a real keener, you can do what Amelia did to dazzle us that day and use a piping bag for perfect café-style striped scones.

CINNAMON BUNS

Makes 6 cinnamon buns

Cinnamon buns, a.k.a. smell paradise, are probably the treat we hear the most talk about. We always sell a lot of these cinn-ful little sweethearts, but never more than we do on Christmas Eve. People buy them by the dozen to reheat in the oven on Christmas morning, giving them something to look forward to after all the gifts are opened and the stockings are inside out. You can make these the night before and store them, unbaked, covered in plastic wrap in the refrigerator. Bake as directed the next morning, letting them come to room temperature before baking.

TIP: *Roll up your sleeves for this one! This recipe is a bit involved, so I strongly encourage, nay, insist, that you read the recipe through before you start. This is so you can have a little foresight into what you'll be doing and hopefully avoid any mishaps.*

Buns

3¾ cups Bob's Red Mill gluten-free all-purpose flour

⅓ cup organic sugar

1 tablespoon xanthan gum

1 teaspoon gluten-free baking powder

½ teaspoon sea salt

1 tablespoon regular active dry yeast

½ cup lukewarm water

¾ cup canned coconut milk

¼ cup Earth Balance Buttery Sticks (½ stick), melted

¼ cup unsweetened applesauce

2 tablespoons + 1½ teaspoons canola oil

1 teaspoon apple cider vinegar

1 teaspoon vanilla extract

Cinnamon Sugar

¼ cup organic sugar

¼ cup Sucanat

2 tablespoons ground cinnamon

1 tablespoon Earth Balance Buttery Sticks, melted

Sauce

¼ cup Earth Balance Buttery Sticks (½ stick), melted

½ cup Sucanat

¼ cup agave nectar

¼ cup canned coconut milk

1 teaspoon vanilla extract

⅛ teaspoon sea salt

Topping

1 batch cream cheese frosting (page 229)

Preheat the oven to 350°F. Have a 9-inch ungreased cake pan ready (the sides should be about 2½ to 3 inches high). Melt all the butter for the recipe—a total of ½ cup + 1 tablespoon. Set aside.

For the buns: In a large bowl, sift together the flour, sugar, xanthan gum, baking powder, and salt. Whisk to combine.

(continued on page 40)

In a small bowl or measuring cup, add the yeast to the warm water (it should feel just slightly warmer than the inside of your wrist). Set aside to let the yeast proof—about 10 minutes or until the yeast is frothy and bubbly.

In a medium bowl, whisk together the coconut milk, melted butter, applesauce, oil, vinegar, and vanilla.

Once the yeast has proofed, stir the yeast mixture into the wet ingredients and then add the combined wet ingredients to the dry ingredients. Stir thoroughly with a spatula until a sticky but firm, well-blended dough is achieved.

For the cinnamon sugar: In a medium bowl, combine the sugar, Sucanat, and cinnamon. Stir in 1 tablespoon melted butter and set aside.

For the sauce: In a small bowl or measuring cup (with a spout for easy pouring), combine the remaining ¼ cup melted butter, Sucanat, agave nectar, coconut milk, vanilla, and salt. Set aside.

Grab two big sheets of parchment paper (about 12 inches long). Spray one side of each sheet with canola oil. Turn out the dough onto one of the oiled sheets, then spray the dough with canola oil. Form the dough into a rough rectangular shape. Place the other sheet of parchment paper over top, oiled side down. Using your hands or a rolling pin, flatten the dough into a rectangular shape, about 8 × 10 inches. Slowly peel back the top parchment paper and set aside.

Sprinkle the cinnamon sugar onto the dough and, using your hands, spread it out to cover the dough edge to edge. Using oiled or wet hands, slowly roll up the dough starting from a shorter side of the rectangle.

Cut the dough roll in half using a sharp knife that has been lightly oiled with canola oil, then cut each half into three rolls. Place the rolls in the cake pan, cut sides up. Pour the prepared sauce evenly over top.

Let the rolls rise for about 10 minutes (don't worry if nothing drastic happens; gluten-free goodies tend to rise mostly in the oven), then bake for 20 minutes or until the tops are firm and a bit golden and the sauce is bubbly. If the sides of the cake pan aren't very high, place a baking sheet beneath the cake pan to catch any sauce that bubbles over. Remove the buns from the oven and let rest for 5 minutes, then flip the cake pan upside down onto a baking sheet or plate. Using a thin, sharp knife, gently separate the buns. Place them on a serving plate before finishing with cream cheese frosting. Serve with coffee and a smile.

MUFFINS

Muffins hold a special place in my sweet little baked-goods heart. While developing our original set of recipes, and long before we opened the bakery's doors, I worked endlessly to achieve the texture and taste that make muffins so irresistible. Our muffins have a devoted following and have even been voted Best Muffins in Toronto. Now you can bake up a nice hot tray of muffins in your very own kitchen and, unlike me, you won't have to swat Kev away when he tries to sneak one before they hit the shelves.

Sweet Potato–Cranberry Muffins 47

Lemon-Blueberry Corn Muffins 49

Apple-Cinnamon Buckwheat Muffins 53

Banana Chocolate-Chip Muffins 55

Chocolate Zucchini Muffins 57

Gingerbread Carrot Muffins 59

Lemon Poppyseed Muffins 61

Pumpkin Chocolate-Chip Muffins 63

SWEET POTATO–CRANBERRY MUFFINS

Makes 12 muffins

This is the mack daddy of muffins at our bakery. For the first few months it was the only muffin we made, and now if we try to skip a day there's a serious outcry from our morning-weary, muffin-loving customers. The combination of sweet potato, cinnamon, and dried tart cranberries is not only delicious but also beautiful. We chose sweet potato as an egg substitute because it has excellent binding properties and a high moisture content, keeping these muffins moist and tender. As an added bonus, it's high in vitamins B6, C, and D, as well as in iron and stress-busting magnesium. What a great way to start your day!

1¾ cups Bob's Red Mill gluten-free all-purpose flour

1¼ cups organic sugar

1 tablespoon gluten-free baking powder

1 tablespoon ground cinnamon

½ teaspoon xanthan gum

¼ teaspoon sea salt

1 cup canned sweet potato purée

½ cup non-dairy milk or water

½ cup canola oil

1 cup dried cranberries

Preheat the oven to 375°F. Line a 12-cup muffin pan with paper liners or spray each muffin cup with canola oil. In a large bowl, sift the flour, then add the sugar, baking powder, cinnamon, xanthan gum, and salt. Whisk thoroughly. In a medium bowl, whisk together the sweet potato, non-dairy milk, and oil. Pour the wet ingredients into the dry ingredients and mix well using a spatula. Fold in the cranberries and let the batter sit for 10 to 15 minutes.

Scoop the batter into the prepared muffin cups to about two-thirds full. Bake for 20 minutes or until a toothpick inserted in the centre of a muffin comes out clean. Let cool for 15 minutes before turning out onto a cooling rack.

LEMON-BLUEBERRY CORN MUFFINS

Makes 12 muffins

Cornmeal makes the texture of these muffins so enjoyable, and the pairing of the subtle lemon flavour and the bright blueberries makes this recipe a real winner. As a bonus, these muffins are lightly sweetened, so if you omit the lemon and blueberries, you will have a simple cornbread muffin that goes great alongside your favourite veggie chili or stew.

1 cup Bob's Red Mill all-purpose gluten-free flour

1 cup cornmeal

½ cup organic sugar

1 tablespoon gluten-free baking powder

½ teaspoon xanthan gum

½ teaspoon sea salt

¾ cup unsweetened applesauce

½ cup canola oil

½ cup rice milk

1 teaspoon vanilla extract

1 teaspoon lemon extract

1 cup fresh or frozen blueberries, tossed lightly in flour

Preheat the oven to 400°F. Line a 12-cup muffin pan with paper liners or spray each muffin cup with canola oil. In a large bowl, sift the flour, then add the cornmeal, sugar, baking powder, xanthan gum, and salt. Whisk thoroughly. In a medium bowl, mix together the applesauce, oil, milk, and vanilla and lemon extracts. Pour the wet ingredients into the dry ingredients and mix well using a spatula. Fold in the blueberries, being careful not to overmix or crush the berries, as they will turn the batter grey. Tossing them in a bit of flour first helps prevent them from discolouring the batter, plus it gives the blueberries a bit of grip so they don't all sink to the bottom.

Scoop the batter into the prepared muffin cups to about two-thirds full. Bake for 20 minutes or until a toothpick inserted in the centre of a muffin comes out clean. Let cool for 15 minutes before turning out onto a cooling rack.

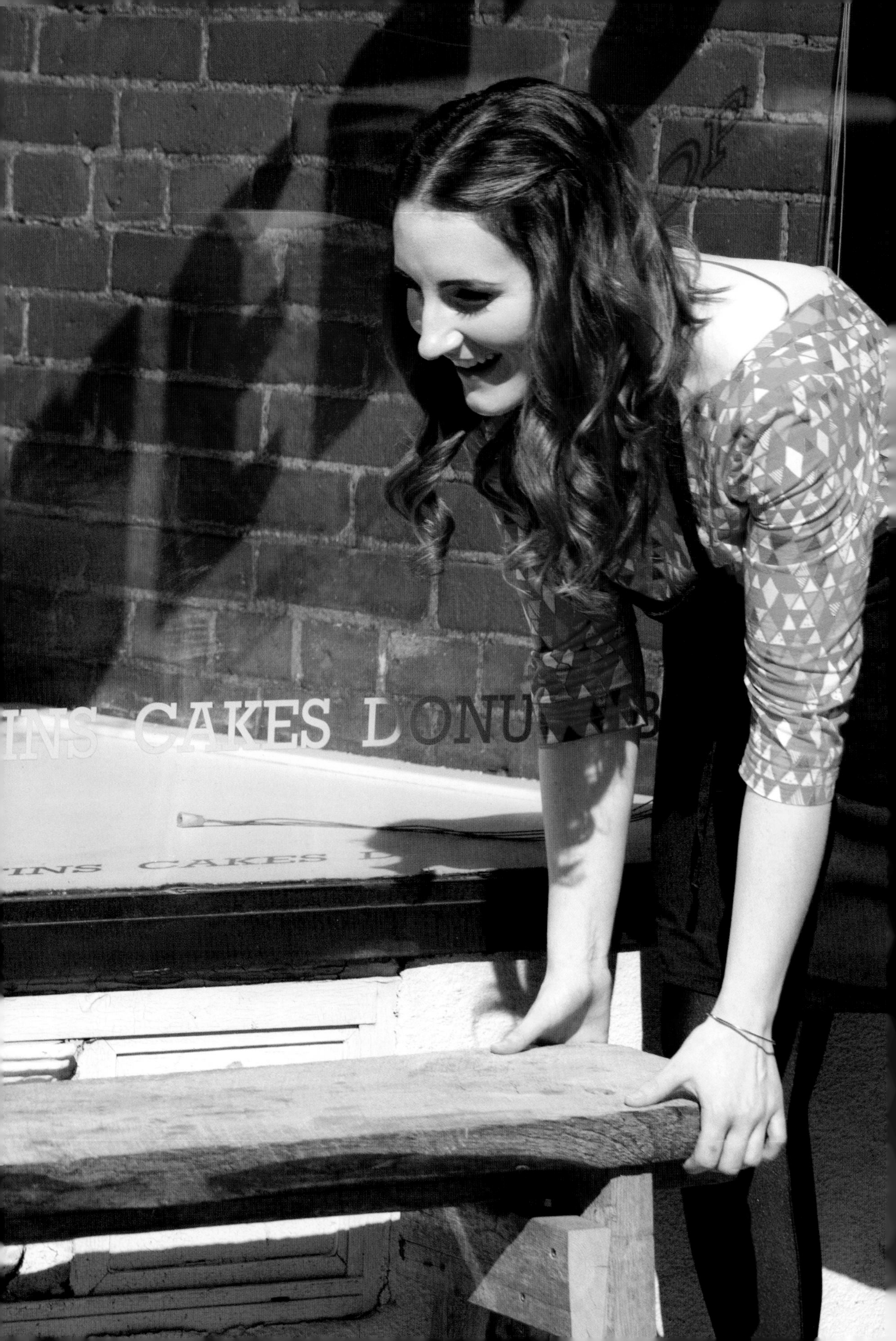
INS CAKES DONU

APPLE-CINNAMON BUCKWHEAT MUFFINS

Makes 12 muffins

Among all the flavour pairings in the world, apple and cinnamon stand out as true soulmates. They really shine together in this muffin, and the buckwheat flour, something we don't often use at the bakery, lends a nuttiness and a really tender crumb. You want to make sure you're using a firm and tart apple here, like a classic Granny Smith, or something more current, like a Pink Lady or Honeycrisp, otherwise the apple flavour will be weak and the texture mealy. I leave the apples unpeeled to get all the vitamin goodness and healthy fibre of the skin but, of course, you can peel them if you prefer.

1 cup Bob's Red Mill gluten-free all-purpose flour	¼ teaspoon ground nutmeg
¾ cup buckwheat flour	1 cup unsweetened applesauce
1¼ cups organic sugar	½ cup rice milk
2 tablespoons ground cinnamon	½ cup canola oil
1 tablespoon gluten-free baking powder	1 tablespoon vanilla extract
½ teaspoon xanthan gum	1 cup cored and chopped apples (¼-inch chunks)
¼ teaspoon sea salt	

Preheat the oven to 400°F. Line a 12-cup muffin pan with paper liners or spray each muffin cup with canola oil.

In a large bowl, sift both flours with the sugar, cinnamon, baking powder, xanthan gum, salt, and nutmeg. Whisk thoroughly. In a medium bowl, mix the applesauce, milk, oil, and vanilla. Pour the wet ingredients into the dry ingredients and mix well using a spatula. Fold in the apples. Let the batter sit for 10 to 15 minutes.

Scoop the batter into the prepared muffin cups to about two-thirds full. Bake for 23 to 25 minutes or until a toothpick inserted in the centre of a muffin comes out clean. Let cool for 15 minutes before turning out onto a cooling rack.

BANANA CHOCOLATE-CHIP MUFFINS

Makes 12 muffins

These muffins are quick and easy to make, and they taste and smell great. Banana, chocolate, and cinnamon are such a classic combo, and the smell when they're baking is one of my favourites in the whole world. The result is a tender, aromatic muffin that, when warm, is simply perfect with a pat of vegan butter melting on top—or get extra decadent by spreading on some peanut butter instead.

1¾ cups Bob's Red Mill gluten-free
   all-purpose flour

¾ cup organic sugar

1 tablespoon gluten-free baking powder

1 tablespoon ground cinnamon

½ teaspoon xanthan gum

¼ teaspoon sea salt

½ cup rice milk

½ cup canola oil

1 cup mashed ripe banana (2 to 3 freckled
   bananas)

1 cup vegan semi-sweet chocolate chips

Preheat the oven to 400°F. Line a 12-cup muffin pan with paper liners or spray each muffin cup with canola oil.

In a large bowl, sift the flour, then add the sugar, baking powder, cinnamon, xanthan gum, and salt. Whisk thoroughly. In a medium bowl, mix the milk and oil. Pour the wet ingredients into the dry ingredients and mix well using a spatula. Fold in the banana, then the chocolate chips. Let the batter sit for 10 to 15 minutes.

Scoop the batter into the prepared muffin cups to about two-thirds full. Bake for 20 minutes or until a toothpick inserted in the centre of a muffin comes out clean. Let cool for 15 minutes before turning out onto a cooling rack.

CHOCOLATE ZUCCHINI MUFFINS

Makes 12 muffins

Zucchini muffins are magical to me. It's almost like eating a bowl of salad, while still getting the warm satis-faction of eating a muffin. I know this is faulty reasoning but bear with me. Zucchini has a lot of calcium, iron, and folate, so even though this muffin is not a salad, it's still nice to know you're getting a few extra nutritional goodies along with it. We also added cocoa to this one; once baked, the zucchini is nowhere to be seen. That makes this a great way to sneak some veg into the diet of those picky eaters.

½ cup soy or coconut milk beverage

1 teaspoon apple cider vinegar

1¼ cups Bob's Red Mill gluten-free all-purpose
   flour

½ cup unsweetened cocoa powder

1⅓ cups organic sugar

1 tablespoon gluten-free baking powder

½ teaspoon xanthan gum

¼ teaspoon sea salt

¼ teaspoon baking soda

½ cup unsweetened applesauce

½ cup canola oil

1½ cups shredded zucchini

Preheat the oven to 400°F. Line a 12-cup muffin pan with paper liners or spray each muffin cup with canola oil.

In a small bowl, combine the milk and vinegar. The reaction of these two ingredients raises the acidity of the milk and causes it to thicken somewhat. Set aside for at least 10 minutes to allow the milk to become "buttermilk."

In a large bowl, sift together the flour and cocoa powder, then add the sugar, baking powder, xanthan gum, salt, and baking soda. Whisk thoroughly. In a medium bowl, whisk together the applesauce and oil. Pour the wet ingredients into the dry ingredients, add the buttermilk, and mix well using a spatula. Fold in the zucchini. Let the batter sit for 10 to 15 minutes.

Scoop the batter into the prepared muffin cups to about two-thirds full. Bake for 25 minutes or until a toothpick inserted in the centre of a muffin comes out clean. Let cool for 15 minutes before turning out onto a cooling rack.

GINGERBREAD CARROT MUFFINS

Makes 12 muffins

If you're a gingerbread fan, these are going to be your new go-to muffins. The gingerbread spice blend is spot-on, and we've added a bit of shredded carrot to the mix to give delicious texture. I eat one of these muffins every single Saturday morning to perk me up while I'm getting the bakery set to open with the rest of the staff. I've even boldly suggested that they may be my #1 treat sweetheart!

½ cup soy or coconut milk beverage

1 teaspoon apple cider vinegar

1¾ cups Bob's Red Mill gluten-free
   all-purpose flour

1 cup organic sugar

1 tablespoon gluten-free baking powder

1½ teaspoons ground ginger

½ teaspoon ground cinnamon

½ teaspoon ground nutmeg

¼ teaspoon baking soda

¼ teaspoon xanthan gum

¼ teaspoon sea salt

½ cup pure pumpkin purée

½ cup canola oil

2 tablespoons organic blackstrap molasses

1½ cups shredded organic carrot

Preheat the oven to 400°F. Line a 12-cup muffin pan with paper liners or spray each muffin cup with canola oil.

In a small bowl, combine the milk and vinegar. The reaction of these two ingredients raises the acidity of the milk and causes it to thicken somewhat. Set aside for at least 10 minutes to allow the milk to sour and become "buttermilk."

In a large bowl, sift the flour, then add the sugar, baking powder, ginger, cinnamon, nutmeg, baking soda, xanthan gum, and salt. Whisk thoroughly. In a medium bowl, mix the pumpkin purée, oil, molasses, and buttermilk. Pour the wet ingredients into the dry ingredients and mix well using a spatula. Fold in the carrots. Let the batter sit for 10 to 15 minutes.

Scoop the batter into the prepared muffin cups to about two-thirds full. Bake for 25 minutes or until a toothpick inserted in the centre of a muffin comes out clean. Let cool for 15 minutes before turning out onto a cooling rack.

LEMON POPPYSEED MUFFINS

Makes 12 muffins

Who can resist a sweet lemon muffin with crunchy little poppy seeds thrown in? These guys are superb for packing in lunches, or for serving up to your friends during a coffee date or tea party.

2 cups Bob's Red Mill gluten-free
   all-purpose flour

½ cup organic sugar

1 tablespoon gluten-free baking powder

½ teaspoon xanthan gum

½ teaspoon sea salt

¾ cup rice milk

½ cup canola oil

¼ cup unsweetened applesauce

1 tablespoon lemon extract

2 teaspoons vanilla extract

⅓ cup poppy seeds

Preheat the oven to 400°F. Line a 12-cup muffin pan with paper liners or spray each muffin cup with canola oil. In a large bowl, sift the flour, then add the sugar, baking powder, xanthan gum, and salt. Whisk thoroughly. In a medium bowl, mix together the milk, oil, applesauce, and lemon and vanilla extracts. Pour the wet ingredients into the dry ingredients and mix well using a spatula. Fold in the poppy seeds and let the batter sit for 10 to 15 minutes.

Scoop the batter into the prepared muffin cups to about two-thirds full. Bake for 20 minutes or until a toothpick inserted in the centre of a muffin comes out clean. Let cool for 15 minutes before turning out onto a cooling rack.

PUMPKIN CHOCOLATE-CHIP MUFFINS

Makes 12 muffins

Along with the Sweet Potato–Cranberry Muffins, these guys are the originals. The flavour of the pumpkin combined with the cinnamon, ginger, and nutmeg really pops—not to mention the generous amount of chocolate chips. When we were barely even Bunner's yet, and long before we opened a retail storefront, we took on a few catering jobs. These muffins debuted at an evening gala for a Toronto eco film festival. Just before the doors opened, I posed for a picture with our catering spread. Only ten minutes into the event, I went to check on the table. There was nothing left but crumbs! Scanning the room, I saw dozens of people smiling and nodding as they wiped the chocolate from the corners of their mouths—and more than one purse bulging suspiciously.

1¾ cups Bob's Red Mill gluten-free
    all-purpose flour

1¼ cups organic sugar

1 tablespoon gluten-free baking powder

1 tablespoon ground cinnamon

1 tablespoon ground ginger

½ teaspoon xanthan gum

¼ teaspoon sea salt

1 cup pure pumpkin purée

½ cup rice milk

½ cup canola oil

2 tablespoons organic blackstrap molasses

1 cup vegan semi-sweet chocolate chips

Preheat the oven to 400°F. Line a 12-cup muffin pan with paper liners or spray each muffin cup with canola oil.

In a large bowl, sift the flour, then add the sugar, baking powder, cinnamon, ginger, xanthan gum, and salt. Whisk thoroughly. In a medium bowl, whisk together the pumpkin purée, milk, oil, and molasses. Pour the wet ingredients into the dry ingredients and mix well using a spatula. Fold in the chocolate chips. Let the batter sit for 10 to 15 minutes.

Scoop the batter into the prepared muffin cups to about two-thirds full. Bake for 18 to 20 minutes or until a toothpick inserted in the centre of a muffin comes out clean (a little melted chocolate on the toothpick is okay). Let cool for 15 minutes before turning out onto a cooling rack.

SAVOURIES

Any baker worth her apron has a few savoury tricks up her sleeve. Believe it or not, there are people out there who prefer dinner over dessert. When baking meets savoury cooking, the results are delicious. These recipes are pure comfort food, and the perfect way to bake your way into even the saltiest of hearts. Look forward to baking up some flaky pockets, a delicious show-stopping veggie pot pie, our famous mac and cheese, and even the most elusive gluten-free treat of all: pizza. So roll up those sleeves, don your chef's hat, and let's get to it!

Spicy Cheddar Biscuits 69

Herb & Garlic Biscuits 71

Savoury Pastry 73

Mexi Pockets 75

Pizza Pockets 77

Veggie Pot Pie 79

Mac & Cheese 83

Pizza 85

SPICY CHEDDAR BISCUITS

Makes 8 biscuits

The perfect vegan and gluten-free biscuit was one of the most challenging items I have ever attempted—right up there with banana bread and brownies. I must have tried to make biscuits a dozen times, with not even a glimmer of success. Discouraged, I took to the Bunner's Facebook page and asked our fans what made a perfect biscuit. The resounding response: Moist with a bit of a crumble, a touch of salt, and, somewhat surprisingly, cheddar. Re-inspired, I took to the kitchen and hit the nail on the head. All it took was a little teamwork.

¾ cup soy or coconut milk beverage

2 teaspoons apple cider vinegar

1¼ cups brown rice flour

¾ cup Bob's Red Mill garbanzo and fava flour

2 teaspoons gluten-free baking powder

1 teaspoon sea salt

½ teaspoon xanthan gum

¼ teaspoon baking soda

2 gluten-free chipotle chilies in adobo sauce,
   seeds removed

7 tablespoons Earth Balance Buttery Sticks

¼ cup Daiya cheddar-style shreds

Preheat the oven to 425°F. Line a baking sheet with parchment paper.

In a small bowl, combine the milk and vinegar. The reaction of these two ingredients raises the acidity of the milk and causes it to thicken somewhat. Set aside for at least 10 minutes to allow the milk to become "buttermilk."

In a food processor, pulse both flours with the baking powder, salt, xanthan gum, baking soda, and chipotles a few times to blend.

Add the butter in tablespoon-size chunks and pulse until the mixture takes on a sandy consistency. Slowly add the buttermilk while continuing to pulse the processor. Stop when everything is just combined—don't overmix.

Add the cheddar and pulse 1 to 3 times to scatter the cheese shreds throughout the dough.

Scoop out eight ⅓-cup portions directly onto the prepared baking sheet. Loosely shape each into a biscuit.

Bake for 15 minutes or until the bottom of the biscuits are golden. Let sit for 10 minutes before serving. Excellent served alongside veggie chili.

TIP: If you like a five-alarm hot sauce, don't seed the chipotles (which are jalapeños in adobo sauce). If you prefer a chipotle flavour minus all the crazy heat, you'll want to seed them so they're not so hot.

HERB & GARLIC BISCUITS

Makes 8 biscuits

Biscuits are so versatile. You couldn't ask for a better pal for homemade soup, stew, breakfast tofu scramble, or a Southern-inspired main course with a deep ladle of mushroom gravy. These biscuits pack a hearty dose of garlic and mixed herbs, which really come alive when you warm them up and top with vegan butter. Don't be tempted to use rice milk instead of the soy or coconut milk beverage here. The creamier the milk used, the better.

¾ cup soy or coconut milk beverage

2 teaspoons apple cider vinegar

1¼ cups brown rice flour

¾ cup Bob's Red Mill garbanzo and fava flour

2 teaspoons gluten-free baking powder

2 teaspoons mixed dried herbs (e.g., thyme, sage, marjoram, and oregano)

1 teaspoon sea salt

1 teaspoon garlic powder

1 teaspoon onion powder

½ teaspoon xanthan gum

¼ teaspoon baking soda

7 tablespoons Earth Balance Buttery Sticks

Preheat the oven to 425°F. Line a baking sheet with parchment paper.

In a small bowl, combine the milk and vinegar. The reaction of these two ingredients raises the acidity of the milk and causes it to thicken somewhat. Set aside for at least 10 minutes to allow the milk to become "buttermilk."

In a food processor, pulse both flours with the baking powder, mixed herbs, salt, garlic powder, onion powder, xanthan gum, and baking soda a few times to blend.

Add the butter in tablespoon-size chunks and pulse until the mixture takes on a sandy consistency. Slowly add the buttermilk while continuing to pulse the food processor. Stop when everything is just combined—don't overmix.

Scoop out eight ⅓-cup portions directly onto the prepared baking sheet. Loosely shape each scoop into a biscuit.

Bake for about 15 minutes or until the bottom of the biscuits are golden. Let cool for 10 minutes, then serve with melting butter on top. For a special treat, whip the butter first with chopped fresh herbs.

SAVOURY PASTRY

Makes enough for one 9-inch single pie shell or 6 pockets

Within a month of opening Bunner's, we had customers begging for a range of savoury items. Being a lifelong sweet-toothed gal, it hadn't even occurred to me to make something non-sweet. Kev and I brainstormed for days, imagining all the savoury treats we could bake up, before settling on our now very popular pockets. I had never made a gluten-free pastry before, so it took a bit of trial and error. When finally we produced a pastry that was tasty, flaky, and sturdy, we knew we had a winner.

You can stuff this pastry with our suggested pocket fillings (see pages 75 and 77), or use it to create a magnificent pot pie (page 79). This would also make a nice rustic galette filled with caramelized onions, squash, and fresh sage leaves.

1 cup brown rice flour

1 cup Bob's Red Mill garbanzo and fava flour

⅓ cup arrowroot starch

1 teaspoon xanthan gum

1 teaspoon sea salt

½ cup Earth Balance Buttery Sticks (1 stick), temperature depends on method used

½ cup Earth Balance Shortening Sticks (1 stick), temperature depends on method used

½ cup cold water

To prepare in a food processor:

In a food processor, pulse both flours with the arrowroot starch, xanthan gum, and salt a few times to combine.

Cut cold butter and shortening into 2-inch cubes. Add to the flour mixture one cube at a time as you continue to pulse the processor, until the chunks are no longer visible and the mixture takes on a sandy consistency.

Add the water a splash at a time, continuing to pulse the processor. Once all the water is added, process until everything is combined.

Using a spatula, remove the dough from the processor. Divide it in half (for quicker chilling) and, using your hands, flatten each portion into a disc. Wrap in plastic wrap and refrigerate for at least 1 hour, and up to overnight, before using.

To prepare by hand or with a hand mixer:

Bring the butter and shortening to room temperature. In a bowl, cream together the butter and shortening using a potato masher, fork, or hand mixer. In a separate bowl, whisk together all the dry ingredients.

Gradually incorporate the dry ingredients into the creamed butter mixture, mixing with your hands or a fork. Add the cold water a splash at a time until everything is combined.

Divide the dough in half (for quicker chilling), flatten into discs, and wrap in plastic wrap. Refrigerate for at least 1 hour, and up to overnight, before using.

MEXI POCKETS

Makes 6 pockets

Bunner's Mexi pockets are great little lunch items that you can bake up and then enjoy throughout the week. Turn these into Mexi breakfast pockets by crumbling in firm tofu when you add the peppers. Savour any left-over filling on top of rice, with a scoop each of salsa and guac.

1 batch savoury pastry (page 73)

1 tablespoon olive or canola oil

½ small yellow onion, diced

2 cloves garlic, minced

2 teaspoons chili powder

½ teaspoon ground coriander

½ jalapeño, seeded and minced

½ cup seeded and diced green or red bell pepper

½ cup salsa

1 15-oz can organic black beans, drained and
   rinsed

Sea salt

1 cup Daiya pepperjack-style shreds

Prepare the pastry and let chill in the refrigerator for at least 1 hour.

Heat the oil in a large frying pan over medium-high heat. Add the onions and sauté until translucent, about 10 minutes. Add the garlic and cook, stirring occasionally, for 2 minutes. Add the chili powder, coriander, jalapeño, and peppers and cook, stirring occasionally, for 2 to 3 minutes. Stir in the salsa and black beans and heat through. Add salt to taste, then set mixture aside.

Preheat the oven to 375°F. Line a baking sheet with parchment paper.

Remove the dough from the refrigerator and divide each disc into three portions. On a well-floured surface, roll out one portion into a ¼-inch-thick circle or a rectangle (with a short side facing you).

Place ⅓ cup black bean filling in the centre of the dough. Sprinkle 2 or 3 tablespoons pepperjack on top of the filling. Carefully fold the dough in half, over the filling. Crimp the edges with your fingers or a fork, ensuring the pocket is fully sealed. Using a spatula, gently transfer the pocket to the prepared baking sheet. Repeat with the remaining portions of dough.

Bake for 25 minutes, until the pastry is golden brown. Serve immediately or store in an airtight container in the refrigerator. To reheat, bake at 375°F until a fork inserted into the centre comes out hot, 15 to 20 minutes.

PIZZA POCKETS

Makes 6 pockets

There was a summer in my university days when I basically lived off prepackaged frozen pizza pockets I bought at the grocery store. After that I vowed never to look at a pizza pocket again. That is, until years later, when we invented our savoury vegan pizza pockets, which are, needless to say, much more appealing. They're perfect for freezing so you can just heat them up for lunch at your leisure. The recipe we use at the bakery is quite simple, but you can doll it up any way you like. Whatever you would order on a pizza is what you should stuff into your pizza pocket. But remember to reduce the amount of mushrooms in the recipe to make space for the ingredients you're adding.

1 batch savoury pastry (page 73)

2 cups organic roasted red pepper and tomato sauce

2 cups organic mushrooms, sliced

Optional fillings: **diced onion, minced fresh garlic, fresh basil leaves, sliced olives, sliced green pepper, pineapple chunks**

1 cup Daiya mozzarella-style shreds

Prepare the pastry and let chill in the refrigerator for at least 1 hour.

Preheat the oven to 375°F. Line a baking sheet with parchment paper.

In a large bowl, combine the sauce, mushrooms, and any other fillings of your choice.

Remove the dough from the refrigerator and divide each disc into three even portions. On a well-floured surface, roll out one portion into a ¼-inch-thick circle or a rectangle (with a short side facing you).

Place ⅓ cup prepared filling in the centre of the dough. Sprinkle 2 or 3 tablespoons mozzarella on top of the filling. Carefully fold the dough in half, over the filling. Crimp the edges with your fingers or a fork, ensuring the pocket is fully sealed. Using a spatula, gently transfer the pocket to the prepared baking sheet. Repeat with the remaining portions of dough.

Bake for 25 minutes or until the pastry is a golden brown. Serve immediately or cool and then refrigerate in an airtight container. To reheat, bake at 375°F until a fork inserted into the centre comes out hot, 15 to 20 minutes.

VEGGIE POT PIE

Makes one 9-inch pie

Pot pie is the quintessential cold-weather cure. Warm gravy and delicious veggies, all wrapped up in a golden flaky crust, can warm the coldest heart (and tummy!). We sell these around the holidays, and the feedback from our loyal customers looking for something to show off on their family dinner table is always tremendous. This is the best recipe for a fall or winter potluck. By sharing it, you'll make vegan and gluten-free look as good as we do!

For an added thrill, add canned white beans or a few handfuls of chopped winter greens like collards or kale to the mix at the end.

2 batches savoury pastry (page 73)

2 tablespoons olive or canola oil

1 small yellow onion, diced

2 cloves garlic, minced

1 tablespoon dried rubbed sage

1 tablespoon dried thyme

3 tablespoons gluten-free tamari

¼ cup + 2 tablespoons Bob's Red Mill garbanzo and fava flour

2 cups gluten-free vegetable stock

3 cups frozen mixed vegetables (peas, carrots, corn)

2 cups cubed frozen or freshly roasted butternut squash

1 cup sliced mushrooms

Sea salt

Rice milk, for brushing

Prepare the pastry and let chill in the refrigerator for at least 1 hour.

Meanwhile, in a large saucepan, heat the oil over medium-high heat. Add the onions and sauté for about 10 minutes, until fragrant and somewhat translucent. Add the garlic and sauté for 1 minute, stirring occasionally. Add the sage and thyme, stirring to coat the onions and garlic, then add the tamari. Sprinkle in ¼ cup flour and cook, stirring constantly, for about 2 minutes, until you can smell the toastiness of the flour.

Stir in the stock. Simmer, uncovered, stirring occasionally so the mixture doesn't burn, until it thickens to a gravy-like consistency, 15 to 20 minutes. If needed, add up to 2 tablespoons flour to thicken the mixture even more, and cook for another 5 minutes. Stir in the mixed vegetables, squash, and mushrooms. Salt to taste. Cook for 2 minutes, until the vegetables are heated through, then remove the pan from the heat and let cool slightly.

Preheat the oven to 375°F.

Remove the dough from the refrigerator. Combine 2 discs (one batch) of pastry and, on a well-floured surface, roll out to a circle about ¼ inch thick and 10 inches in diameter. Transfer to a 9-inch glass pie plate by gently rolling the dough around the rolling pin like a jelly roll, then unrolling it onto the pie plate and lightly pressing it down.

(continued on page 80)

Pour the gravy and vegetable mixture into the pie shell. Using a wooden spoon, smooth out the mixture so it's flush with the edge of the pie plate.

On a well-floured surface, roll out the remaining dough to a circle roughly the same size as the first. Using the same rolling method as for the shell, transfer the dough on top of the filling. Trim the overhang and crimp the pastry edges with your fingers or a fork to seal.

Using a pastry brush, lightly brush the pie top with rice milk so that it bakes up with a golden gloss. Bake for 45 minutes on the middle oven rack. Check after 25 minutes. If the top is already a bit too brown, cover it with foil; otherwise leave uncovered for the remaining baking time.

Let rest for about 10 minutes before serving with a salad.

MAC & CHEESE

Makes enough for 2 hungry people, or 4 sides

This dish is so simple, it's almost too good to be true. It's ideal for a weeknight meal: the sauce is a snap to make, and if you're in a real rush, you don't even need to bake it. Throw in some chopped greens like kale or broccoli, or add a smoky kick with a little bit of chopped chipotle. This dish can also be doubled easily if you have a bigger troop of tummies to fill.

8 ounces brown rice elbow pasta

2 tablespoons Earth Balance Buttery Sticks

1¼ cups coconut milk beverage

6 tablespoons nutritional yeast flakes

1 tablespoon fresh lemon juice

2 teaspoons Dijon mustard

1½ teaspoons onion powder

1½ teaspoons garlic powder

1 teaspoon sea salt

Ground black pepper

1 tablespoon arrowroot starch

1 cup Daiya mozzarella-style shreds

1 15-oz can puréed butternut squash (or 1½ cups roasted and puréed squash)

½ cup gluten-free bread crumbs

½ to 1 teaspoon paprika

Preheat the oven to 400°F. Bring a large pot of salted water to boil. Add the pasta and cook according to the package directions.

In a medium saucepan over medium-high heat, melt 1 tablespoon butter. Add the milk, nutritional yeast, lemon juice, mustard, onion powder, garlic powder, salt, and pepper. Whisk briskly to combine. Slowly whisk in the arrowroot starch. Simmer until the sauce begins to thicken, about 5 minutes. Add the mozzarella shreds and slowly whisk until melted, about 5 minutes. Add the squash and whisk until everything is combined and heated through. Add the cooked pasta to the sauce, stirring gently to combine. Season to taste.

Pour the mixture into an ovenproof baking dish—either a 9-inch (round) glass pie plate or a 9- × 9-inch square dish works well.

In a saucepan, melt the remaining butter. Add the bread crumbs and toss to coat well, then sprinkle evenly over the pasta. Top with a sprinkling of paprika.

Bake for 15 minutes or until the sauce begins to bubble. Serve hot with a side salad and ketchup or hot sauce.

PIZZA

Makes two 8-inch pizzas

When the moon hits your eye like a big gluten pie, that's a . . . tummy ache. Well, tummy aches be damned. Bunner's is here to say that pizza doesn't need any gluten at all to bring you to a state of amore.

¾ cup lukewarm water (just slightly warmer
   than the inside of your wrist)

2¼ teaspoons active dry yeast (not instant)

2 teaspoons organic sugar

¼ cup lukewarm water

2 tablespoons ground flaxseed

¾ cup potato starch

½ cup brown rice flour

⅓ cup Bob's Red Mill gluten-free all-purpose flour

⅓ cup tapioca starch

1 teaspoon xanthan gum

1 teaspoon sea salt

1 teaspoon garlic powder

1 teaspoon dried thyme

1 teaspoon dried oregano

½ cup olive oil

Optional toppings: tomato sauce, pesto, Daiya
   mozzarella-style shreds, sliced olives, sundried
   tomatoes, mushrooms, and peppers

Line two baking sheets with parchment paper.

In a small bowl, combine the lukewarm water with the yeast and sugar. Give it a whisk and set aside somewhere warm for 10 minutes or until the yeast proofs, bubbling up and becoming very frothy.

In another small bowl, combine ¼ cup water and flaxseed.

In a large bowl, whisk together the potato starch, both flours, the tapioca starch, xanthan gum, salt, garlic powder, thyme, and oregano. Add the yeast mixture, flaxseed mixture, and oil to the dry ingredients. Using a spatula, mix until you achieve a sticky but fairly firm dough. Divide the dough into two balls.

On a well-floured surface, roll out one of the dough balls until it is as thin as you can make it (about ⅛ inch thick). The dough will be very sticky and won't feel the same as a gluten crust when rolling it out; you'll need to use extra flour and you may want to use your hands to pat it down as thin as possible. Carefully slide the round onto a prepared baking sheet. Repeat with the second dough ball.

Preheat the oven to 400°F. Meanwhile, place the baking sheets on the stovetop to give the crusts a bit of time (and warmth) to rise before baking. The rise isn't significant, but it does improve the texture.

Once the oven is preheated, bake the crusts for 10 to 12 minutes, until the bottoms are slightly golden brown.

Remove from the oven and top with the sauce and toppings of your choice. Bake for another 12 minutes, until the crust is crispy and the toppings are cooked through. The pizzas are best enjoyed the day they're baked.

COOKIES, BARS
& SQUARES

I'm a big fan of portable treats. I ride my little motorcycle nearly everywhere and, well, sometimes you need to bring a treat where no cupcake can go and trust that it will get there intact. That sturdiness also makes cookies and bars ideal for lunchboxes and picnics. So I hope you're wearing two pairs of socks, because this chapter is gonna blow one of them off. The gang's all here! You've got our classic chocolate chip cookies, our famously buttery date squares, our award-winning brownies, plus a few new kicks to try out too, like Nanaimo bars and s'mores. And yes, any and all treats from this chapter make the perfect companion whether you're heading out on a road trip, relaxing at the beach, hiking in a park, or setting off on your next urban adventure.

Chocolate Chip Cookies...91

Double Chocolate-Chip Cookies 93

Oatmeal Raisin Cookies..95

S'more Cookies 97

Brownies...99

Blondies.. 101

Nanaimo Bars 103

Chocolate Chip–Coconut Pretzel Bars..105

Date Squares...107

Maple Fudge 111

CHOCOLATE CHIP COOKIES

Makes 18 cookies or 9 creamies

These cookies were one of my first and biggest successes in the kitchen, and one that I'm still so proud of today. Not only are they fantastic on their own, but using them to sandwich a dollop of vanilla buttercream deliciously transforms these guys into our famous creamies. We also use these cookies to make cookie crumbs for our Nanaimo Bars (page 103), as well to make the crust for our Chocolate Cheesecake (page 145), which may sound unusual, but trust me, they give the cheesecake a toffee-like quality that is simply indulgent.

These cookies are versatile size-wise. You can make them huge or you can shrink them down to little bite-size cuties and they will still turn out. Simply adjust the baking time by a few minutes, give or take, and let visual cues tell you when they're done (they should be a warm golden brown).

2½ cups brown rice flour	¾ cup + 1 tablespoon organic sugar
½ cup potato starch	¾ cup agave nectar
2 tablespoons arrowroot starch	⅓ cup melted coconut oil
1 teaspoon gluten-free baking powder	2 teaspoons vanilla extract
1 teaspoon baking soda	1 teaspoon organic blackstrap molasses
1 teaspoon xanthan gum	⅔ cup vegan semi-sweet chocolate chips
1 teaspoon sea salt	

Preheat the oven to 325°F. Line two baking sheets with parchment paper.

In a large bowl, sift together the flour, both starches, baking powder, baking soda, xanthan gum, and salt. Whisk to combine.

In a medium bowl, whisk together the sugar, agave nectar, oil, vanilla, and molasses.

Add the wet ingredients to the dry ingredients and mix well using a spatula. Fold in the chocolate chips until evenly distributed.

Using your hands, roll the dough into golf-ball-size pieces and place on the prepared baking sheets. Press down to flatten each ball to about ¼ inch thick and 2½ inches in diameter, being mindful to keep them spaced about 1 inch apart.

Bake for 12 to 15 minutes, until golden. Let sit on the baking sheets for at least 20 minutes, to firm up. Transfer to a cooling rack to cool completely, or eat them all right away.

VARIATION

Creamies: Let the cookies cool completely. Dollop 1 tablespoon vanilla buttercream frosting (page 225) on the underside of a cookie. Top with a second cookie, press together to sandwich, and serve.

DOUBLE CHOCOLATE-CHIP COOKIES

Makes 18 cookies or 9 creamies

Double chocolate anything is always an excellent idea. These cookies pair a rich chocolate base with sweet and melty chocolate chips, and are a dream come true if you can never get enough chocolate in your life. With a generous spoonful of vanilla buttercream frosting in between two cookies, these look like big, fresh Oreos.

1¾ cups brown rice flour

¾ cup unsweetened cocoa powder

½ cup potato starch

2 tablespoons arrowroot starch

1 teaspoon gluten-free baking powder

1 teaspoon baking soda

1 teaspoon xanthan gum

1 teaspoon sea salt

¾ cup + 1 tablespoon organic sugar

¾ cup agave nectar

⅓ cup + 1 tablespoon melted coconut oil

2 teaspoons vanilla extract

1 teaspoon organic blackstrap molasses

⅔ cup vegan semi-sweet chocolate chips

Preheat the oven to 325°F. Line two baking sheets with parchment paper.

In a large bowl, sift together the flour, cocoa powder, both starches, baking powder, baking soda, xanthan gum, and salt. Whisk to combine.

In a medium bowl, whisk together the sugar, agave nectar, oil, vanilla, and molasses.

Add the wet ingredients to the dry ingredients and mix well using a spatula. Fold in the chocolate chips until evenly distributed.

Using your hands, roll the dough into golf-ball-size pieces and place on the prepared baking sheets. Press down to flatten each cookie to about ¼ inch thick and 2½ inches in diameter, being mindful to keep them spaced about 1 inch apart.

Bake for 12 to 15 minutes or until the cookies begin to look more matte than glossy. Let sit on the baking sheets for at least 20 minutes, to firm up. Transfer to a cooling rack to cool completely, or eat them all right away.

VARIATION

Creamies: Let the cookies cool completely. Dollop 1 tablespoon vanilla buttercream frosting (page 225) on the underside of a cookie. Top with a second cookie, press together to sandwich, and serve.

OATMEAL RAISIN COOKIES

Makes 12 cookies

I love oatmeal raisin cookies, so it's surprising to me that it took writing this cookbook to bring one to our menu. Once I hit upon the perfect formulation for this soft and chewy cookie, I couldn't stop taste-testing them—I was head over heels! I know some of you may not be into raisins (for reasons I can't possibly fathom), so I guess you could substitute chocolate chips instead. Or you can do both if you want to be extra sassy, adding ½ cup chocolate chips in with ½ cup raisins.

1 cup gluten-free oats

1 cup Bob's Red Mill gluten-free all-purpose flour

½ cup organic sugar

¼ cup ground flaxseed

1½ teaspoons ground cinnamon

1 teaspoon sea salt

½ teaspoon xanthan gum

¾ cup canola oil

⅓ cup soy or coconut milk beverage

1 teaspoon vanilla extract

1 cup Thompson raisins

Preheat the oven to 350°F. Line a baking sheet with parchment paper.

In a large bowl, mix the oats, flour, sugar, flaxseed, cinnamon, salt, and xanthan gum until well combined.

In a medium bowl, whisk together the oil, milk, and vanilla. Add the wet ingredients to the dry ingredients and mix well using a spatula. Fold in the raisins.

Using a scant ¼-cup measure, roll out 12 balls of dough and place on the prepared baking sheets. Press down to flatten each cookie to about ¼ inch thick and 2½ inches in diameter, being mindful to keep them spaced about ½ inch apart.

Bake for 15 minutes or until the tops firm up and are golden brown. Let sit on the baking sheets for at least 20 minutes, to firm up. Transfer to a cooling rack to cool completely.

S'MORE COOKIES

Makes 18 cookies

Kevin has this thing where he tells me something unbelievable and, being completely and unwaveringly gullible, I always believe it. When we first started dating he told me he had never heard of the movie Babe. Not that he hadn't seen it—that he hadn't even heard of it. Understandably, I freaked out. About a year ago, Kev told me he had never heard of a s'more. I was incredulous, and because we were camping, I cobbled together what turned out to be a very disappointing, lukewarm s'more-ish monster. I'm still not sure if his claim was true, but these cookies are delicious. As vegans, it's difficult for us to find gelatin-free marshmallows and honey-free graham crackers, so a s'more is really something to behold. Vegan marshmallows can be found in most health food stores, and we're forgoing the graham crackers altogether by making our own cookie.

2½ cups brown rice flour

½ cup potato starch

2 tablespoons arrowroot starch

1 teaspoon xanthan gum

1 teaspoon gluten-free baking powder

1 teaspoon baking soda

1 teaspoon sea salt

1 teaspoon ground cinnamon

¾ cup + 1 tablespoon organic sugar

¾ cup agave nectar

⅓ cup melted coconut oil

2 teaspoons vanilla extract

1 teaspoon organic blackstrap molasses

1 cup vegan semi-sweet chocolate chips

1 cup vegan mini marshmallows or quartered full-size vegan marshmallows

Preheat the oven to 325°F. Line two baking sheets with parchment paper.

In a large bowl, sift together the flour, both starches, xanthan gum, baking powder, baking soda, salt, and cinnamon. Whisk to combine.

In a medium bowl, whisk together the sugar, agave nectar, oil, vanilla, and molasses. Add the wet ingredients to the dry ingredients and mix well using a spatula, hand mixer, or stand mixer. Fold in the chocolate chips to evenly distribute. Fold in the marshmallows.

Using your hands, roll the dough into golf-ball-size pieces and place on the prepared baking sheets. Flatten each ball to about ¼ inch thick and 2½ inches in diameter, being mindful to keep them spaced about 1 inch apart.

Bake for 12 to 15 minutes, until the cookies are a warm, golden brown and the marshmallows look somewhat melted. Let sit on the baking sheets for at least 20 minutes, to firm up. Transfer to a cooling rack to cool completely.

VARIATION

Rocky Road Cookies: Add ½ cup chopped almonds along with the marshmallows, and reduce the chocolate chips to ½ cup.

BROWNIES

Makes 12 brownies

If you've ever been to the bakery, chances are you've been coerced into trying one of our deliciously rich brownies. Our staff all have their favourite treats, of course, but everyone can agree that the brownie is a must-have.

This recipe was a labour of love and took us several tasty experiments over two years to develop. Our efforts were not in vain, though, as we have developed what we think are the best brownies on the planet. A perfect balance of fudgy and cakey, decadently rich and packing a potent chocolate punch, these brownies are one of our most loved creations. The secret is in the applesauce, which replaces the eggs and makes these tasty treats tender, moist, and cholesterol-free to boot.

These are especially yummy served with coconut milk ice cream (try crumbling the brownie on top), and make the perfect crumbled topping for our oh-so-decadent Chocolate Cheesecake (page 145).

1 cup Bob's Red Mill gluten-free all-purpose flour

¾ cup unsweetened cocoa powder

1 cup Sucanat

1 cup organic sugar

½ teaspoon gluten-free baking powder

½ teaspoon xanthan gum

½ teaspoon sea salt

1 cup unsweetened applesauce

½ cup canola oil

¾ cup vegan semi-sweet chocolate chips

Preheat the oven to 350°F. Spray a 12-cup muffin pan with canola oil.

In a large bowl, sift together the flour and cocoa powder, then whisk in the Sucanat, sugar, baking powder, xanthan gum, and salt.

In a separate bowl, mix together the applesauce and oil. Add the wet ingredients to the dry ingredients and mix well. Fold in the chocolate chips.

Pour ⅓ cup batter into each prepared muffin cup. Bake for 30 to 35 minutes, until the tops are firm and slightly shiny. (Testing for doneness with a toothpick may not work here thanks to the melted chocolate chips inside and the tenderness of the cake.) Let cool for 15 minutes before removing from the muffin pan with a butter knife. Store in an airtight container in the refrigerator.

VARIATIONS

Mint Brownies: Add ½ teaspoon peppermint extract along with the chocolate chips.

Peanut Butter Brownies: After distributing the batter in the muffin cups, swirl 2 teaspoons peanut butter into each.

Raspberry Brownies: Replace ¼ cup applesauce with ¼ cup mashed raspberries.

Walnut Brownies: Add ¼ cup chopped walnuts along with the chocolate chips.

BLONDIES

Makes 12 blondies

Blondies are the vanilla version of a brownie. Yes, I know that the brownie is a tried, true, and tested Bunner's bestseller, but before you start to scoff, trust me when I say that a blondie is no ditzy stereotype and can hold its own against its cocoa-rich, valedictorian classmate.

Now, we don't need to convince our fellow vanilla lovers out there that vanilla is anything but boring. Remember those vanilla Girl Guide cookies? Exactly. You politely thanked the little Guide on your porch, closed the door on her a little too abruptly, and then tore open the package. Well, I think you'll feel the same type of excitement as your blondies bake, filling your home with that sweet classic vanilla smell. So next time you're feeling kind of meh on chocolate, give these little ladies a whirl and see for yourself if blondies do, in fact, have more fun.

1¾ cups Bob's Red Mill gluten-free
    all-purpose flour

2 cups organic sugar

½ teaspoon gluten-free baking powder

½ teaspoon xanthan gum

½ teaspoon sea salt

1 cup unsweetened applesauce

½ cup canola oil

1 teaspoon vanilla extract

½ cup vegan semi-sweet chocolate chips

Preheat the oven to 350°F. Spray a 12-cup muffin pan with canola oil.

In a large bowl, sift the flour, then whisk in the sugar, baking powder, xanthan gum, and salt. In a separate bowl, mix together the applesauce, oil, and vanilla. Add the wet ingredients to the dry ingredients and mix well. Fold in the chocolate chips.

Pour ¼ cup batter into each prepared muffin cup. Bake for 30 to 35 minutes, until the tops are firm and slightly shiny. (Testing for doneness with a toothpick may not work here thanks to the melted chocolate chips inside and the tenderness of the cake.) Let cool for 15 minutes before removing from the muffin pan with a butter knife. Store in an airtight container in the refrigerator.

NANAIMO BARS

Makes 12 squares

These rich and sugary little squares pop up at potluck family functions and church basements everywhere. Originally from Nanaimo, British Columbia, this bar is steeped in mystery and intrigue. Some say it was a housewife who first submitted the recipe for publication in the 1950s. Others say it dates back to the 1930s or even the 1800s. Whatever the origins, it's ours now!

Bottom Layer

½ cup Earth Balance Buttery Sticks (1 stick), melted

⅓ cup unsweetened cocoa powder

¼ cup organic sugar

1 teaspoon vanilla extract

2 cups chocolate chip cookie crumbs (use your favourite brand of cookies or our recipe, page 91)

1 cup unsweetened shredded coconut

Middle Layer

¼ cup Earth Balance Buttery Sticks (½ stick), chilled

1¾ cups organic powdered sugar, sifted

¼ cup vegan custard powder*

3 tablespoons canned coconut milk

1 teaspoon vanilla extract

Top Layer

½ cup vegan semi-sweet chocolate chips

1 tablespoon canola oil

Line a 9- × 9-inch glass baking dish with parchment paper.

For the bottom layer: In a large bowl, whisk together the melted butter, cocoa powder, sugar, and vanilla. Fold in the cookie crumbs and coconut until evenly distributed. Press the mixture into the bottom of the prepared baking dish and refrigerate for 1 hour.

For the middle layer: Using a hand mixer, cream the butter, gradually adding the powdered sugar, custard powder, coconut milk, and vanilla. Evenly spread the mixture over the chilled base, then refrigerate for 30 minutes.

For the top layer: Using a double boiler, melt the chocolate chips over medium heat, stirring every few minutes. Ensure you don't get any water in them or the chocolate will seize up and turn chunky. Once the chocolate is melted and silky, stir in the oil until well combined. Slowly pour the chocolate over the top layer, being careful not to make it too thick in any one area. Using a spatula, gently spread the chocolate over the entire surface. Refrigerate for another 30 minutes.

Once the slab is cooled and firmed up, cut it into 12 squares. Store in an airtight container in the refrigerator.

* If you can't find vegan custard powder, substitute with ¼ cup arrowroot starch and increase the vanilla to 2 teaspoons.

CHOCOLATE CHIP– COCONUT PRETZEL BARS

Makes one 9- × 12-inch tray or 12 squares

The combination of salty and sweet is one that has always appealed to me—salted caramel and salty peanuts on top of a hot fudge sundae, even chocolate-covered potato chips! At the bakery, we don't use nuts so that our establishment is friendly for nearly every diet and allergy. As a result, we have to brainstorm more creative ways to get that salty crunch into something soft and sweet. Enter pretzels. In this new world where vegan and gluten-free options abound, finding gluten-free pretzels should be a cinch (check at a health-food store or an online supplier). If, however, you can't, sub in a nut of your choice; pecans or peanuts are both good options.

2 cups chocolate chip cookie crumbs (use your favourite brand of cookies or our recipe, page 91)

½ cup melted coconut oil

1 can (400 mL) full-fat coconut milk

⅔ cup Sucanat

1½ cups vegan semi-sweet chocolate chips

2 cups sweetened shredded coconut

2 cups gluten-free salted pretzels, broken into nickel-size pieces

Preheat the oven to 350°F. Line a 9- × 12-inch glass baking pan with parchment paper.

In a large bowl and using your hands, combine the cookie crumbs and oil. Press the mixture into the bottom of the prepared baking pan.

In a saucepan over medium heat, whisk together the coconut milk and Sucanat. Reduce the heat and simmer for 10 to 15 minutes, whisking often, until the mixture has reduced slightly. Pour over the cookie base in the baking dish.

Sprinkle the chocolate chips evenly over the milk mixture, then top with an even layer of coconut followed by an even layer of pretzels. Being mindful of the hot milk, press down these ingredients with your hands until evenly covered. Bake for 30 minutes, until lightly browned and bubbling. Let cool for 1 hour, then refrigerate overnight or for at least 8 hours.

Using a sharp knife, cut these babies into 12 squares. Store in an airtight container in the refrigerator.

DATE SQUARES

Makes 12 home-size squares or 8 Bunner's-size squares

Did you know that the great Egyptian pharaoh Tutankhamen was buried with a hearty supply of dates? Could it be he was planning a trip to Bunner's in the afterlife? Well, this square was one of Kevin's first requests when I was experimenting with new recipes, and really, who doesn't love this classic and classy king of the squares family? Buttery golden oats sandwiching rich, silken dates . . . by this description, our tasty date square would fit right in beside King Tut's most decadent riches!

I really love how simple and easy this recipe is. The longest step for us at the bakery is pitting the dates. That said, you will need a food processor for this recipe, so if you don't have one, now's the time to part with some of that royal gold and invest.

3 cups pitted dates	½ teaspoon baking soda
1 cup water	¼ teaspoon sea salt
2 cups gluten-free oats	⅛ teaspoon ground cinnamon
1 cup Bob's Red Mill gluten-free all-purpose flour	1 cup Earth Balance Buttery Sticks (2 sticks),
¾ cup organic sugar	chilled and cut into large chunks

Preheat the oven to 350°F. Spray a 9- × 9-inch baking dish with canola oil.

In a medium saucepan, combine the dates and water and bring to a boil. Reduce the heat and simmer for about 5 minutes. Remove from the heat and let cool.

In a food processor, pulse the oats, flour, sugar, baking soda, salt, and cinnamon about 10 times, until coarsely chopped—you don't want to overprocess it. Add half the butter and pulse about 10 times. Add the remaining butter and pulse until the mixture starts coming together and pulls away from the sides of the work bowl.

Set aside one-third of the mixture in a bowl. Using your hands, scoop the remaining two-thirds into the prepared baking dish, pressing firmly and evenly to form the base. Wet your hands before spreading if you find the mixture too sticky to work with.

Transfer the cooled dates to the food processor and process to a smooth, thick paste. Using a spatula, spread the dates evenly over the prepared base. Sprinkle the remaining oat mixture on top of the dates. They will form a nice crumble over top but won't completely cover the dates. Using your hands, lightly press down the crumble topping.

Bake for 30 minutes. Let cool completely, then refrigerate for 8 hours. Using a sharp knife, cut into 12 regular-size or 8 large squares and store in an airtight container in the refrigerator.

MAPLE FUDGE

Makes about sixty-four 1-inch pieces

Keeping small-town tourism alive one nibble at a time, and populating charming little farmers' markets across the land, thick slabs of maple fudge are enchantingly rural. Really, you can't get more Canadian than this.

The recipe is a bit trickier than most, and through the ups and downs of developing it, I discovered that a hand mixer and a candy thermometer are worth their weight in golden maple fudge. Use the best dark maple syrup you can get your hands on. And if you're not a nut-free household, adding 1 cup chopped walnuts is the perfect counterpart to this smooth and sugary delight.

1 cup organic sugar

1 cup Sucanat

1 cup canned coconut milk

5 tablespoons Earth Balance Buttery Sticks

¼ cup dark maple syrup

Pinch baking soda

½ teaspoon vanilla extract

Spray a large mixing bowl and an 8-inch square baking dish (a loaf pan would do in a pinch) with canola oil.

In a medium saucepan over medium heat, combine the sugar, Sucanat, coconut milk, butter, maple syrup, and baking soda. Bring to a gentle boil and cook, stirring often, for about 10 minutes or until the mixture hits the soft ball stage on a candy thermometer (about 230°F). If you don't have a candy thermometer, test that the fudge is ready by spooning a bit of the boiling mixture into a bowl of ice water. If the mixture comes together into a soft, pliable ball, it's ready. If it stays liquid, you need to boil it longer, and if it seems pretty hard, you may have boiled it too long and will have to start over.

When the mixture has hit the soft ball stage, immediately pour it into the prepared mixing bowl, but resist the urge to scrape down the sides or the bottom of the pan—this can lead to sandy-feeling fudge. Add the vanilla. Using a hand mixer on low speed, gently beat the mixture for 10 to 15 minutes, until it has lost its super-glossy sheen and is much thicker. If you are adding walnuts, now's the time.

Using a spatula, scrape the thickened mixture into the prepared baking dish. Let cool at room temperature for at least 4 hours, and up to overnight, until set. Using a sharp knife, slice the fudge into 1-inch squares and store in an airtight container.

DONUTS

D onuts, usually enveloped in cinnamon sugar or dipped in some delicious concoction, are a coveted treat at the bakery because we make them only on Saturdays, as a novel weekend attraction. That's not to say that people aren't asking for them all week long; it's just that you can't do everything every day, and some treats just have to wait their turn. This chapter, along with a couple of donut pans, is your ticket to making the perfect baked donut on any day you see fit. Make sure you try your best (I know it's difficult) to eat these donuts the same day that you make them. They don't do very well sealed up in a container and, like all donuts, just taste better the day of.

Cinnamon Sugar Donuts...117

Toasted Coconut Donuts...119

Glazed Chocolate Donuts 121

The Lumberjack 123

CINNAMON SUGAR DONUTS

Makes 12 donuts

The donut that inspired a generation! Well, maybe not, but people certainly love this delicious sweetheart. When Kev redid our website last year and wrote new copy for all the products, the tagline for the donut went viral. With a simple "I love you, little donut," he melted the heart of every donut lover out there. It's true, our unassuming donut is often overlooked for the more obvious treats in the crowd, but once you give it a chance, you'll understand why we and so many others have such a soft spot for this shy little classic.

2 cups + 2 tablespoons Bob's Red Mill gluten-free all-purpose flour

¾ cup + 2 tablespoons organic sugar

2¼ teaspoons gluten-free baking powder

¾ teaspoon xanthan gum

¾ teaspoon sea salt

¾ cup + 2 tablespoons rice milk

½ cup unsweetened applesauce

1 tablespoon canola oil

1 teaspoon vanilla extract

½ teaspoon lemon extract

Cinnamon Sugar

½ cup organic sugar

½ teaspoon ground cinnamon

Preheat the oven to 325°F. Spray two 6-mould donut pans or one 12-mould donut pan with canola oil.

In a large bowl, sift the flour, then add the sugar, baking powder, xanthan gum, and salt. Whisk to combine.

In a medium bowl, whisk together the milk, applesauce, oil, and vanilla and lemon extracts. Pour the wet ingredients into the dry ingredients and mix well. Batter should be smooth, with no lumps, so that your donut is less craggy and more puffy. Use the batter immediately, as the donuts will be dense if the batter sits too long.

Scoop ¼ cup batter into each donut mould (it should be full). Bake for 11 to 13 minutes, until a very light golden brown. Let cool for 10 minutes before removing from the pans.

For the cinnamon sugar: In a medium bowl, whisk together the sugar and cinnamon.

After turning the slightly cooled donuts out of the pans, spray the side of the donut that was exposed in the oven with a bit of canola spray (the other side should already be slightly moist). Using your hands, toss both sides of each donut in the cinnamon sugar. Eat the same day.

TOASTED COCONUT DONUTS

Makes 12 donuts

What's better than our original Cinnamon Sugar Donuts (page 117)? Well, it's a matter of preference, of course, but if you love filling your kitchen with the aromatic fragrance of coconut shavings toasting in the oven as much as we do, then Toasted Coconut may win the medal for donut of the month in your kitchen. This divine donut is dunked in a coconut-infused glaze and then dipped in oven-toasted coconut shavings to give it a warm, golden glow. Its sprinkles are au naturel! For a quick and colourful pink twist, swap out the toasted coconut for raw coconut shavings tossed with a few drops of beet juice or red food dye.

1 batch cinnamon sugar donuts (page 117)
(omit cinnamon sugar topping)

Toasted Coconut

¾ cup unsweetened shredded coconut

Vanilla Dip

1 tablespoon Earth Balance Buttery Sticks

1½ cups organic powdered sugar, sifted 2 tablespoons non-dairy milk (preferably coconut milk beverage)

1 tablespoon vanilla extract

Prepare the donuts and let cool for 10 minutes before removing from the pans.

To toast the coconut: Preheat the oven to 350°F. Spread the coconut evenly over the bottom of a cake pan or a baking sheet and bake for 5 minutes. Remove from the oven, give it a good stir, and then bake until golden and fragrant, checking every 2 minutes to ensure the coconut doesn't burn. Transfer to a flat plate.

For the vanilla dip: Heat a frying pan over medium heat. Melt the butter, then whisk in the sugar, milk, and vanilla, whisking continuously until the mixture is smooth and somewhat thick.

Using your hands, dip one side of each donut in the vanilla dip, then dip the glazed side into the toasted coconut, coating thoroughly. Place on a cooling rack with a sheet of parchment paper beneath to catch drips. Let set for 10 minutes. Eat the same day.

GLAZED CHOCOLATE DONUTS

Makes 12 donuts

As an electrician, my dad has been his own boss for 30 years. It seems like every time I talk to him he's wiring up a new Tim Hortons, and I wouldn't be surprised if he's wired nearly every single one of them in St. Catharines (the Tim Hortons capital of Canada). When I was growing up, he used to bring home tons of different types of donuts, but my absolute faves were the chocolate ones. I suspect that my love of all things baked came from my daily (daily!) treat delivery from my dad; I know he's the source of my entrepreneurial spirit. So when you're sitting down to a hot coffee and this homemade chocolate donut, you have Jim Wittig to thank for it.

1½ cups + 2 tablespoons Bob's Red Mill
    gluten-free all-purpose flour

½ cup unsweetened cocoa powder

¾ cup + 2 tablespoons organic sugar

2¼ teaspoons gluten-free baking powder

¾ teaspoon xanthan gum

¾ teaspoon sea salt

¾ cup + 2 tablespoons rice milk

½ cup unsweetened applesauce

1 tablespoon canola oil

1½ teaspoons vanilla extract

1 batch donut glaze (page 237)

Preheat the oven to 325°F. Spray two 6-mould donut pans or one 12-mould donut pan with canola oil.

In a large bowl, sift together the flour and cocoa powder, then add the sugar, baking powder, xanthan gum, and salt. Whisk to combine.

In a medium bowl, whisk together the milk, applesauce, oil, and vanilla. Pour the wet ingredients into the dry ingredients and mix well. The batter should be smooth, with no lumps, so that your donut is less craggy and more puffy. Use the batter immediately, as the donuts will be dense if the batter sits too long.

Scoop ¼ cup batter into each donut mould (it should be full). Bake for 14 to 16 minutes. Let cool for 10 minutes before removing from the pans.

Make glaze. Using your hands, dip one side of each donut in the glaze and place on a cooling rack with a sheet of parchment paper beneath to catch drips. Let set for 10 minutes. Serve or, if you must, store in an airtight container in the refrigerator.

THE LUMBERJACK

Makes 12 donuts

The Lumberjack first appeared as a one-time offering at a vegan bake-off, yet woodsmen are rumoured to still tell the tale of its existence. Yes, returning to camp from a hard day's work, the giants of pioneer lore might have snickered at a tray of strawberry cupcakes. But they would have quickly dropped their axes and called "Timber!" to fell one of Bunner's legendary Lumberjack donuts. Dripping with a hearty dose of Canadiana, this donut is first topped with a sweet maple glaze and then dipped in crispy vegan "bacon." This recipe takes a little time and finesse, so clear the wood chips and get ready to test your strength and endurance.

1 batch cinnamon sugar donuts (page 117)
   (omit cinnamon sugar topping)

Smoked Coconut Bacon

1 cup unsweetened flaked coconut (not shredded)

2 tablespoons water

2 tablespoons melted coconut oil

2 tablespoons maple syrup

2 tablespoons apple cider vinegar

2 tablespoons gluten-free tamari

1 tablespoon paprika

1 teaspoon garlic powder

½ teaspoon liquid smoke (optional)

Maple Dip

1 tablespoon Earth Balance Buttery Sticks

1½ cups organic powdered sugar, sifted

2 tablespoons maple syrup

1 tablespoon vanilla extract

Pinch sea salt

For the smoked coconut bacon: In a container that won't stain or absorb odours (a Mason jar works well), combine the flaked coconut, water, oil, maple syrup, vinegar, tamari, paprika, garlic powder, and liquid smoke (if using). Shake gently to thoroughly mix without breaking up the coconut flakes too much. Let the mixture marinate for at least 1 hour at room temperature.

Prepare the donuts and let cool for 10 minutes before removing from the pans.

Heat a large frying pan over medium-high heat. While the pan is heating, strain the coconut, discarding the marinade. Spray the hot pan lightly with canola oil, then add the coconut to the pan. Cook for 5 to 10 minutes, using a wooden spoon or metal spatula to push around the coconut "bacon," being careful to not let it burn. Remove the coconut from the heat as soon as the sides become a bit dark and crispy around the edges, placing on a plate lined with several sheets of paper towel. Break up the coconut a bit as it cools if it sticks together.

For the maple dip: In a frying pan over medium heat, melt the butter, then whisk in the sugar, maple syrup, and vanilla until smooth and somewhat thick.

Using your hands, dip one side of each donut in the maple dip and place on a cooling rack with a sheet of parchment paper beneath to catch drips. Sprinkle coconut bacon on top. Best served same day.

CAKES

A gorgeously decorated cake means one thing and one thing only: party time. I often find myself sending out a freshly frosted cake and imagining people standing around *oohing* and *aahing* as it's cut. Or singing "Happy Birthday" as someone makes a wish and blows out the candles. Since the cakes we make at the bakery are exclusively for celebration purposes, making them is such a positive process, and we pour extra love into every step, from batter to frosting.

We've included lots of lovely cake options in this chapter, from a simple pound cake (page 143) for tea parties to my favourite, the tricked-out Ashley's Delight Cake (page 139), a banana-berry cake dream.

Birthday Cake... 129

Chocolate Cake 131

Red Velvet Cake 133

Strawberry Cake 135

Ashley's Delight Cake... 139

Pound Cake 143

Chocolate Cheesecake.. 145

BIRTHDAY CAKE

Makes one 9-inch double-layer cake

This cake is at the epicentre of Bunner's birthday-ness. It basically spells "Happy Birthday" in rainbow frosting. Every year, Kevin and I celebrate our birthdays a mere four days apart, and every year we make a giant vanilla cake with chocolate frosting to thank our amazing customers. This people-pleaser is the only cake you'll need on your birthday, not just because everyone will love it but because the most important person at the party will—you!

1½ cups brown rice flour

1½ cups Bob's Red Mill garbanzo and fava flour

⅓ cup potato starch

¼ cup arrowroot starch

1½ tablespoons gluten-free baking powder

2 teaspoons sea salt

½ teaspoon baking soda

½ teaspoon xanthan gum

1½ cups agave nectar

1 cup + 2 tablespoons canola oil

¾ cup unsweetened applesauce

¾ cup rice milk

3 tablespoons vanilla extract

2 batches chocolate buttercream frosting
   (page 227)

Preheat the oven to 375°F. Spray two 9-inch cake pans with canola oil.

In a large bowl, sift both flours and starches with the baking powder, salt, baking soda, and xanthan gum. Whisk well to combine.

In a medium bowl, whisk together the agave nectar, oil, applesauce, milk, and vanilla. Pour the wet ingredients into the dry ingredients and mix together.

Divide the batter evenly between the prepared cake pans. Bake for 30 minutes or until a knife or toothpick inserted into the centre of a cake comes out clean.

Let the cakes cool to room temperature, then wrap them, still in the pans, in plastic wrap and refrigerate for at least 2 hours, and up to overnight.

When you're ready to frost the cake, remove from the pans and place the bottom layer on a serving plate. Spread with one-third of the chocolate buttercream frosting. Place the second layer on top and cover the entire cake with the remaining frosting. (See page 220 for detailed frosting instructions.)

CHOCOLATE CAKE

Makes one 9-inch double-layer cake

Everyone loves a big slice of rich chocolate cake, which is why this is one of our most popular cakes at the bakery. We use a beautiful blend of fluffy gluten-free flours, rich fair-trade organic cocoa, and pure organic golden agave nectar to make this cake the showstopper that it is.

1 cup unsweetened cocoa powder

1 cup brown rice flour

1 cup Bob's Red Mill garbanzo and fava flour

⅓ cup potato starch

¼ cup arrowroot starch

2 teaspoons sea salt

1½ teaspoons gluten-free baking powder

½ teaspoon baking soda

½ teaspoon xanthan gum

1½ cups agave nectar

1⅓ cups canola oil

¾ cup unsweetened applesauce

¾ cup rice milk

3 tablespoons vanilla extract

2 batches chocolate buttercream frosting

   (page 227)

Preheat the oven to 375°F. Spray two 9-inch cake pans with canola oil.

In a large bowl, sift the cocoa powder with both flours and starches, salt, baking powder, baking soda, and xanthan gum. Whisk well to combine.

In a medium bowl, whisk together the agave nectar, oil, applesauce, milk, and vanilla. Pour the wet ingredients into the dry ingredients and mix well, scraping down the bottom and sides of the bowl as necessary.

Divide the batter evenly between the prepared cake pans. Bake for 30 minutes or until a knife or toothpick inserted in the centre of a cake comes out clean.

Let the cakes cool to room temperature, then wrap both cakes, still in their pans, in plastic wrap and refrigerate for at least 2 hours, and up to overnight.

When you're ready to frost the cake, remove from the pans and place the bottom layer on a serving plate. Spread with one-third of the chocolate buttercream frosting. Place the second layer on top and cover the entire cake with the remaining frosting. (See page 220 for detailed frosting instructions.)

VARIATIONS

Cookies and Cream Chocolate Cake: Replace the chocolate frosting with vanilla buttercream frosting (page 225). After frosting the bottom layer, crumble 2 to 3 double chocolate-chip cookies (page 93) on top of the frosting. Then cover the entire cake with the remaining frosting.

Mocha Cake: Replace the rice milk with ¾ cup cold brewed coffee.

RED VELVET CAKE

Makes one 9-inch double-layer cake or 18 cupcakes

Red velvet cake stirs the romantic imagination. Flowing gowns on the dance floor of the Waldorf Astoria; a nervous young valentine saying, "Will you be mine?"; your grandmother's hand-stitched wedding dress on the biggest day of your life. Red velvet cake evokes a certain sensuality that makes most other cakes blush.

Red velvet has a chocolate flavour, but the origins of its colour are contested. One theory is pure science experiment: When it was originally developed in the American South, just the right blend of acidic vinegar and buttermilk would react with a certain kind of cocoa powder to release anthocyanin, a water-soluble pigment that would turn the cake a modest but pronounced shade of red. The other theory is a little more practical: During the Second World War, food rationing forced bakers to use plentiful beet juice to both enhance the colour of their cakes and help retain their moisture.

These days, a rich cream cheese frosting is paired with this tender, moist cake to create an enchanting and memorable experience that will complement any occasion calling for a show-stopping centrepiece on the dessert table.

1 cup soy or coconut milk beverage	1½ cups organic sugar
1 tablespoon apple cider vinegar	½ cup unsweetened applesauce
1½ cups Bob's Red Mill garbanzo and fava flour	7 tablespoons canola oil
⅔ cup potato starch	2 tablespoons fresh beet juice or red food dye
⅓ cup arrowroot starch	1 tablespoon vanilla extract
2 tablespoons unsweetened cocoa powder	2 batches cream cheese frosting (page 229) or
1 teaspoon baking soda	vanilla buttercream frosting (page 225)
½ teaspoon xanthan gum	
½ teaspoon sea salt	

Preheat the oven to 350°F. Spray two 9-inch cake pans with canola spray.

In a small bowl, combine the milk and vinegar. The reaction of these two ingredients raises the acidity of the milk and causes it to thicken somewhat. Set aside for at least 10 minutes to allow the milk to become "buttermilk."

In a large bowl, sift together the flour, both starches, cocoa powder, baking soda, xanthan gum, and salt. Add the sugar and whisk thoroughly.

In a medium bowl, whisk together the applesauce, oil, beet juice, and vanilla. Add the wet ingredients to the dry ingredients, then pour in the buttermilk. Using a spatula, mix thoroughly. Let the batter sit for 10 minutes.

Evenly divide the batter between the prepared cake pans. Bake for 25 minutes or until a toothpick or a knife inserted in the centre of a cake comes out clean.

(continued on page 134)

Let the cakes cool to room temperature, then wrap them, still in their pans, in plastic wrap and refrigerate for at least 2 hours, and up to overnight.

When you're ready to frost the cake, remove from the pans and place the bottom layer on a serving plate. Spread with one-third of the frosting of your choice. Place the second layer on top and cover the entire cake with the remaining frosting. (See page 220 for detailed frosting instructions.)

VARIATION

Josephine Louise Snack Cake: In lunchbox snack-cake land, one king ruled them all. Here's how to make our all-natural version of a beloved childhood favourite.

Make the red velvet cake batter as directed, but instead of doling it out into cake pans, make little cakes, as if for whoopie pies, by scooping ¼ cup batter directly onto two baking sheets lined with parchment paper. Repeat with the remaining batter, spacing cakes about 2 inches apart. Bake at 350°F for 10 to 15 minutes, until a knife or toothpick inserted in the centre of a cake comes out clean. Cool completely on the baking sheet.

Meanwhile, melt ½ cup vegan semi-sweet chocolate chips in a double boiler over medium heat, stirring every few minutes. (If you don't have a double boiler, use a heatproof measuring cup placed in a saucepan filled with 1 to 2 inches of water.) Be sure not to splash any water on the chocolate or it will seize up and turn chunky. Once the chocolate is melted and silky, remove from the heat.

Sandwich a generous dollop of vanilla buttercream frosting (page 225) between two of the little cakes and place on a piece of parchment. Once you have assembled the pies, drizzle the tops with the melted chocolate (using a fork or piping bag) and let set in the refrigerator for 20 minutes.

STRAWBERRY CAKE

Makes one 9-inch double-layer cake

The cake equivalent of a sweet summer romance—vanilla cake with fresh organic strawberries folded into the batter, lots of ripe sliced strawberries between the layers, generously wrapped in a dreamy vanilla buttercream frosting. As with most of our recipes, you can customize this cake by replacing the strawberries with your favourite berries. Just make sure you have the same volume of purée (not just cups of loose berries).

1½ cups Bob's Red Mill garbanzo and fava flour

¾ cup potato starch

⅓ cup + 1 tablespoon arrowroot starch

1 tablespoon gluten-free baking powder

1½ teaspoons sea salt

¾ teaspoon xanthan gum

¼ teaspoon baking soda

1 cup agave nectar

¾ cup rice milk

½ cup + 1 tablespoon puréed strawberries (about 10 to 12 fresh)

½ cup canola oil

2 tablespoons + 1 teaspoon vanilla extract

2 batches vanilla buttercream frosting (page 225)

1 cup sliced fresh strawberries

Preheat the oven to 325°F. Spray two 9-inch cake pans with canola oil.

In a large bowl, sift together the flour, both starches, baking powder, salt, xanthan gum, and baking soda. Whisk the ingredients together thoroughly.

In a medium bowl, whisk together the agave nectar, milk, strawberry purée, oil, and vanilla. Add to the dry ingredients. Using a spatula, mix the batter well, then let it sit for about 10 minutes to rise.

Evenly divide the batter between the prepared cake pans. Bake for 30 minutes or until a toothpick or a knife inserted in the centre of a cake comes out clean. The cake will be a bit golden on the sides, and you will be able to smell the strawberries.

Let the cakes cool to room temperature, then wrap them, still in their pans, in plastic wrap and refrigerate for at least 2 hours, and up to overnight.

When you're ready to frost the cake, remove from the pans and place the bottom layer on a serving plate. Spread with one-third of the vanilla buttercream, then scatter the strawberries over top. Place the second layer on top and cover the entire cake with the remaining frosting. (See page 220 for detailed frosting instructions.)

VARIATIONS

Blueberry Cake: Replace the strawberries with blueberries, and frost with cream cheese frosting (page 229).

Raspberry Cake: Replace the strawberries with raspberries, and keep it light with lemon buttercream frosting (page 233).

ASHLEY'S DELIGHT CAKE

Makes one 9-inch double-layer cake

Yes, it's my favourite cake in the world! Right alongside birthday cake, red velvet cake, cheesecake, pound cake, strawberry cake . . . you get the idea. I'm kind of into cake.

A sweet and tender banana cake topped with a special strawberry frosting—it's to die for. Banana baking in the oven is also one of my favourite smells, so again, it's just all of Ashley's greatest hits up in here. If you have another berry preference, you can change up the jam in the frosting recipe, but trust me, strawberry is the best.

1½ cups brown rice flour

1½ cups Bob's Red Mill garbanzo and fava flour

⅓ cup potato starch

¼ cup arrowroot starch

1½ tablespoons gluten-free baking powder

2 teaspoons sea salt

½ teaspoon baking soda

½ teaspoon xanthan gum

1½ cups agave nectar

1 cup + 2 tablespoons canola oil

¾ cup rice milk

¾ cup mashed ripe banana (2 or 3 freckled
   bananas)

3 tablespoons vanilla extract

1 batch strawberry-jam buttercream frosting

Strawberry-Jam Buttercream Frosting

1 cup Earth Balance Buttery Sticks (2 sticks),
   at room temperature

1 cup Earth Balance Shortening Sticks (2 sticks),
   at room temperature

7 cups organic powdered sugar, sifted

½ cup strawberry jam of your choice

1 tablespoon vanilla extract

2 to 3 tablespoons canned coconut milk or soy
   creamer (if needed)

Preheat the oven to 375°F. Spray two 9-inch cake pans with canola oil.

For the cake: In a large bowl, sift both flours and starches with the baking powder, salt, baking soda, and xanthan gum. Whisk well to combine.

In a medium bowl, whisk together the agave nectar, oil, milk, banana, and vanilla. Pour the wet ingredients into the dry ingredients and mix well.

Divide the batter evenly between the two baking pans and bake for 30 minutes or until a knife or toothpick inserted in the centre of a cake comes out clean. Let the cakes cool to room temperature in their pans, then wrap them, still in the pans, in plastic wrap and refrigerate for at least 2 hours, and up to overnight.

For the strawberry-jam buttercream: Using a stand mixer or hand mixer, cream together the butter and shortening until smooth and fluffy. Slowly add the sugar, mixing well. Add the jam and vanilla. If needed to achieve a nice, spreadable consistency, add the coconut milk, 1 tablespoon at a time, and mix well

Whip the frosting for several minutes, until fluffy. Use immediately or store in the refrigerator. If refrigerated, bring to room temperature and give it a good turn with a frosting spatula or butter knife before frosting the cake.

When you're ready to frost the cake, remove from the pans and place the bottom layer on a serving plate. Spread with one-third of the strawberry-jam buttercream. Place the second layer on top and cover the entire cake with the remaining frosting. (See page 220 for detailed frosting instructions.)

TIP: This cake also tastes amazing frosted with maple buttercream (page 235).

POUND CAKE

Makes one 9- × 5-inch loaf

When we were brainstorming new recipes for this cookbook, this one was one the first, and a dream treat of Kevin's. He had the vision in his head of a traditional yellow pound cake with a lightly browned surface. As a child, he had eaten plenty of these with his family and was determined that we make one that looked and tasted exactly the same as those in his fond memories. I, on the other hand, had never had a pound cake in my life, so I had him explain to me every nuance of taste and texture before heading into the kitchen with my sleeves rolled up. When I emerged hopeful, pound cake in hand, I was delighted to see his face light up, and as it turns out, this also became one of my favourite recipes in the book. The ingredients may seem heavy on the coconut, but that doesn't translate through to the taste at all, though its richness substitutes for the dense buttery flavour of a traditional pound cake.

½ cup soft silken tofu

1¼ cups organic sugar

¾ cup coconut milk beverage

½ cup plain or vanilla coconut yogurt

½ cup melted coconut oil

2 teaspoons vanilla extract

1 teaspoon lemon extract

2¼ cups Bob's Red Mill gluten-free all-purpose flour

1½ teaspoons gluten-free baking powder

½ teaspoon baking soda

½ teaspoon xanthan gum

½ teaspoon sea salt

Preheat the oven to 325°F. Spray a 9- × 5-inch loaf pan with canola oil.

In a food processor, purée the tofu until it's completely smooth. Add the sugar, coconut milk, yogurt, oil, and vanilla and lemon extracts and pulse to combine.

In a medium bowl, sift together the flour, baking powder, baking soda, xanthan gum, and salt and add to the tofu mixture. Mix until the dough comes together—about 1 minute. The dough will be very thick.

Using a spatula, scoop the dough into the prepared loaf pan and smooth flat.

Bake for 1 hour, or until a toothpick inserted in the centre of the cake comes out clean. Remove from oven and let cool in pan. Cool completely before slicing.

VARIATION

Jam Swirl Pound Cake: After scooping the dough into the prepared loaf pan, use a knife to swirl ¼ cup of your favourite jam into it.

CHOCOLATE CHEESECAKE

Makes one 8-inch cheesecake

The first time I test-baked this cheesecake at the bakery, the staff were enchanted. It's rich and thick like a true cheesecake should be and, somehow, the crust made out of the chocolate chip cookies tastes almost like a toffee chocolate bar. Of course, you could also use our Double Chocolate-Chip Cookies (page 93) for the crust and it would be equally delicious, not to mention that you would be able to boast about having made a double chocolate cheesecake (or would it be a triple?). There are quite a few combinations possible here to motivate you to make this chocolate wonder time and again.

Crust

1½ cups chocolate chip cookie crumbs (use your
   favourite brand of cookies or our recipe,
   page 91)

⅓ cup melted coconut oil

Filling

1 cup vegan semi-sweet chocolate chips

2 tablespoons melted coconut oil

2 8-oz tubs Tofutti non-hydrogenated vegan
   cream cheese

½ cup organic sugar

2 tablespoons agave nectar

1 tablespoon unsweetened cocoa powder

2 teaspoons vanilla extract

¼ teaspoon sea salt

1 batch chocolate ganache (page 241) (optional)

Preheat the oven to 325°F. Spray an 8-inch springform pan with canola oil.

For the crust: In a large bowl, combine the cookie crumbs and oil. Mix with a fork, until the crumb mixture holds its shape when squeezed together. Using your hands, press the crumb mixture evenly over the base of the springform pan to create the crust.

For the filling: In a double boiler, melt the chocolate chips over medium heat, stirring every few minutes. (If you don't have a double boiler, use a heatproof measuring cup placed in a saucepan filled with 1 to 2 inches of water.) Be sure not to splash any water on the chocolate or it will seize up and turn chunky. Once the chocolate is melted and silky, remove from the heat. Stir in the oil, then let cool for 5 to 10 minutes.

In a food processor, combine the cooled chocolate, cream cheese, sugar, agave nectar, cocoa powder, vanilla, and salt, scraping down the sides of the work bowl as necessary. Using a spatula, scoop the filling onto the prepared crust and smooth it evenly over top.

Bake for 30 minutes, then turn off the oven and let the cake rest in the hot oven for another 30 minutes. Chill the cheesecake in the refrigerator for 3 hours, and up to overnight. *(continued on page 146)*

To remove the cake from the pan, run a sharp knife around the edge before releasing the sides of the springform pan. If using ganache, spread a thin layer on top of the cheesecake before serving. Let set in the refrigerator for 20 minutes. Then slice and serve.

VARIATIONS

Brownie-Caramel Chocolate Cheesecake: Omit the ganache. Crumble 1 to 2 brownies (page 99) (about 1 cup) and sprinkle on top of the cheesecake. Drizzle with caramel sauce (page 239).

"Light" Chocolate Cheesecake: Substitute 1 package of cream cheese with 1 package of firm silken tofu to make a creamier, less dense cheesecake.

Zebra-Striped Cheesecake: Instead of topping the cheesecake with ganache, use a piping bag filled with donut glaze (page 237) to make smart zebra-like stripes on top of the cake.

CUPCAKES

Cupcakes are a thing of simple and selfish beauty. They're not like a cake that you might have to share, slice by slice (the horror!), but rather a singular little treat that you keep all to yourself. Fluffy, delicate, and topped with a nice creamy frosting, cupcakes are the revered princess diamonds in our display case. All the recipes here are for 18 cupcakes, but if you're the polite sort who's into sharing, each recipe can also be easily turned into a double-layered 9-inch cake (just up the baking time to about 30 minutes).

Chocolate Cupcakes 153

Vanilla Cupcakes 155

Lemon Cupcakes 157

Caramel Cupcakes 159

Mexican Chocolate Cupcakes 161

French Toast Cupcakes 165

CHOCOLATE CUPCAKES

Makes 18 cupcakes

I've always been an avid vanilla girl, but this cupcake has made me a chocolate disciple. Topped with chocolate buttercream, it's absolute heaven. But don't let that stop you from getting creative and topping it with whatever frosting you please, or transforming it altogether into a Fauxstess cupcake (see the variation below).

1⅓ cups Bob's Red Mill garbanzo and fava flour

¾ cup unsweetened cocoa powder

6 tablespoons potato starch

3 tablespoons arrowroot starch

1 tablespoon gluten-free baking powder

1½ teaspoons sea salt

½ teaspoon xanthan gum

¼ teaspoon baking soda

1 cup agave nectar

¾ cup canola oil

¾ cup rice milk

½ cup + 1 tablespoon unsweetened applesauce

2 tablespoons vanilla extract

1 batch chocolate buttercream frosting (page 227) (2 batches if using a piping bag for big swirls of frosting)

Preheat the oven to 325°F. Line 18 muffin cups (you'll need two 12-cup muffin pans) with paper liners.

In a large bowl, sift together the flour, cocoa powder, both starches, baking powder, salt, xanthan gum, and baking soda. Whisk to combine.

In a medium bowl, whisk together the agave nectar, oil, milk, applesauce, and vanilla. Add the wet ingredients to the dry ingredients. Using a spatula, thoroughly mix the batter, then let sit for about 10 minutes to rise.

Pour batter into each liner to about two-thirds full. Bake for 20 to 24 minutes, until a knife or toothpick inserted in the centre of a cupcake comes out clean. Cool completely at room temperature before frosting.

VARIATIONS

Ice-Cream Sandwiches: Scoop the batter into ice cream–sandwich baking moulds, or scoop ¼ cup batter directly onto a parchment-lined baking sheet, spacing cakes about 2 inches apart. Bake at 325°F for 10 to 15 minutes, until a toothpick or knife inserted in the centre of a cake comes out clean. Cool completely on the baking sheet.

Gently remove a cake from the baking sheet and dollop with 2 tablespoons softened ice cream. Sandwich between another cake. Repeat with the remaining cakes. Eat right away or freeze, to enjoy throughout the week.

Fauxstess: Once the baked cupcakes have cooled, core out a little hole in the centre of each cupcake about the width of a nickel and about halfway into the cupcake. Using a teaspoon, fill with vanilla buttercream frosting (page 227). Tuck a little bit of the cut-out cake back into the top of the hole, and dip in chocolate ganache (page 241). Let set in the refrigerator. Get extra fancy by piping a little curlicue on the top with the leftover vanilla buttercream.

VANILLA CUPCAKES

Makes 18 cupcakes

The most versatile cupcake in all the land, the vanilla cupcake is the true universal cupcake base. You can pretty much do anything you want with this cupcake and it will taste amazing. Top it with any of the frostings in this book and enjoy all the different flavours of the cupcake spectrum! You can add flavour extracts or fillings if you wish (see the instructions for filling cupcakes in the Caramel Cupcakes recipe, page 159). That said, in my opinion, nothing is better than a fresh vanilla cupcake frosted with creamy vanilla buttercream. It's total perfection in its simplicity.

1½ cups Bob's Red Mill garbanzo and fava flour

¾ cup potato starch

⅓ cup + 1 tablespoon arrowroot starch

1 tablespoon ground cinnamon

1 tablespoon gluten-free baking powder

1½ teaspoons sea salt

¾ teaspoon xanthan gum

¼ teaspoon baking soda

1 cup agave nectar

¾ cup rice milk

½ cup + 1 tablespoon unsweetened applesauce

½ cup canola oil

2 tablespoons vanilla extract

1 batch vanilla buttercream frosting (page 225)
(2 batches if using a piping bag for big swirls of frosting)

Preheat the oven to 325°F. Line 18 muffin cups (you'll need two 12-cup muffin pans) with paper liners.

In a large bowl, sift together the flour, both starches, cinnamon, baking powder, salt, xanthan gum, and baking soda. Whisk to combine.

In a medium bowl, whisk together the agave nectar, milk, applesauce, oil, and vanilla. Add the wet ingredients to the dry ingredients. Using a spatula, thoroughly mix the batter, then let it sit for about 10 minutes to rise.

Pour batter into each liner to about two-thirds full. Bake for 20 to 24 minutes, until a knife or toothpick inserted in the centre of a cupcake comes out clean. The cupcakes will be lightly golden on top.

Cool completely at room temperature before frosting with vanilla buttercream.

VARIATION

Pumpkin Pie Cupcakes: Replace the applesauce with pumpkin purée and add 1 tablespoon pumpkin pie spice to the dry ingredients. These taste especially good with our cream cheese frosting (page 229).

LEMON CUPCAKES

Makes 18 cupcakes

There's nothing quite like a citrus kick to brighten your day. Make these for your best friend when he's feeling blue and watch him light up like a ray of sunshine as he sinks his teeth into this zesty, lemon zinger. A guaranteed day-picker-upper.

1½ cups Bob's Red Mill garbanzo and fava flour

¾ cup potato starch

⅓ cup + 1 tablespoon arrowroot starch

1 tablespoon gluten-free baking powder

1½ teaspoons sea salt

¾ teaspoon xanthan gum

¼ teaspoon baking soda

1 cup agave nectar

¾ cup rice milk

½ cup + 1 tablespoon unsweetened applesauce

½ cup canola oil

2 tablespoons vanilla extract

1 tablespoon lemon extract

1 batch lemon buttercream frosting (page 233)
 (2 batches if using a piping bag for big swirls of
 frosting)

5 lemon slices, cut into quarters, for garnish

Preheat the oven to 325°F. Line 18 muffin cups (you'll need two 12-cup muffin pans) with paper liners.

In a large bowl, sift together the flour, both starches, baking powder, salt, xanthan gum, and baking soda. Whisk to combine.

In a medium bowl, whisk together the agave nectar, milk, applesauce, oil, and vanilla and lemon extracts. Add the wet ingredients to the dry ingredients. Using a spatula, thoroughly mix the batter, then let it sit for about 10 minutes to rise.

Pour batter into each liner to about two-thirds full. Bake for 20 to 24 minutes, until a knife or toothpick inserted in the centre of a cupcake comes out clean. The cupcakes will be lightly golden on top.

Cool completely at room temperature before frosting with lemon buttercream. If desired, garnish each cupcake with a small wedge of lemon just before serving.

CARAMEL CUPCAKES

Makes 18 cupcakes

Caramel is one of the more elusive vegan treats out there, and at the bakery, many a daydream has revolved around the soft, sweet sauce being poured onto various treats. Pulled straight from fantasy to beautiful reality, this is our vanilla cupcake with a soft, creamy caramel filling and a decadent caramel frosting. For an easy salted caramel variation, simply sprinkle the top of each cupcake with a pinch of fleur de sel.

1 batch caramel sauce (page 239)

1½ cups Bob's Red Mill garbanzo and fava flour

¾ cup potato starch

⅓ cup + 1 tablespoon arrowroot starch

1 tablespoon gluten-free baking powder

1½ teaspoons sea salt

¾ teaspoon xanthan gum

¼ teaspoon baking soda

1 cup agave nectar

¾ cup rice milk

½ cup + 1 tablespoon unsweetened applesauce

½ cup canola oil

2 tablespoons vanilla extract

1 batch caramel buttercream frosting (2 batches if using a piping bag for big swirls of frosting)

Caramel Buttercream Frosting

½ cup Earth Balance Buttery Sticks (1 stick), at room temperature

½ cup Earth Balance Shortening Sticks (1 stick), at room temperature

3½ cups organic powdered sugar, sifted

1 teaspoon vanilla extract

5 tablespoons caramel sauce (page 239)

Non-dairy milk (if needed)

Preheat the oven to 325°F. Line 18 muffin cups (you'll need two 12-cup muffin pans) with paper liners. Prepare the caramel sauce and keep in the refrigerator until ready to use.

For the cupcakes: In a large bowl, sift together the flour, both starches, baking powder, salt, xanthan gum, and baking soda. Whisk to combine.

In a medium bowl, whisk together the agave nectar, milk, applesauce, oil, and vanilla. Add the wet ingredients to the dry ingredients. Using a spatula, thoroughly mix the batter, then let it sit for about 10 minutes to rise.

Pour batter into each liner to about two-thirds full. Bake for 20 to 24 minutes, until a knife or toothpick inserted in the centre of a cupcake comes out clean. The cupcakes will be slightly golden on top. Cool completely at room temperature before frosting.

For the caramel buttercream: Using a stand mixer or hand mixer, cream together the butter and short-ening until smooth and fluffy. Slowly add the sugar, mixing well. Add the vanilla and caramel sauce. If needed to achieve a nice, spreadable consistency, add a splash of a non-dairy milk. Whip the frosting for several minutes,

(continued on page 160)

until fluffy. Use immediately or store in the refrigerator. If refrigerated, bring to room temperature and give it a good turn with a frosting spatula or butter knife before using.

To fill the cupcakes, use a paring knife to carve out a tunnel in each cupcake about the width of a nickel and about halfway into the cupcake. Using a teaspoon, fill each hole with as much caramel sauce as the cupcake will hold. Frost with caramel buttercream and drizzle each cupcake with about 1 tablespoon caramel sauce.

MEXICAN CHOCOLATE CUPCAKES

Makes 18 cupcakes

In my life before Bunner's, I was a sales director for a natural cosmetics company, taking care of the shops in Toronto. I used to call the shop managers my little mijas (daughters), and I originally had named this cupcake the Mija because it was spicy like they were. A rich chocolate cupcake, laced with cinnamon and cayenne, similar to how the Mayans are said to have enjoyed their chocolate when they first discovered it. Now every time I eat one of these cupcakes, I remember my little mijas and all the feisty fiestas we had.

TIP: *The cayenne in this recipe has a lot of flavour but not a lot of heat. If you like things* muy caliente*, double the cayenne.*

1⅓ cups Bob's Red Mill garbanzo and fava flour

¾ cup unsweetened cocoa powder

6 tablespoons potato starch

3 tablespoons arrowroot starch

2 tablespoons ground cinnamon

1 tablespoon cayenne pepper

1 tablespoon gluten-free baking powder

1½ teaspoons sea salt

½ teaspoon xanthan gum

¼ teaspoon baking soda

1 cup agave nectar

¾ cup + 3 tablespoons rice milk

¾ cup canola oil

½ cup + 1 tablespoon unsweetened applesauce

2 tablespoons vanilla extract

1 batch cinnamon buttercream chocolate frosting (2 batches if using a piping bag for big swirls of frosting)

Cinnamon Chocolate Buttercream Frosting

½ cup Earth Balance Buttery Sticks (1 stick), at room temperature

½ cup Earth Balance Shortening Sticks (1 stick), at room temperature

3½ cups organic powdered sugar, sifted

¾ cup unsweetened cocoa powder, sifted

1 tablespoon ground cinnamon

1 teaspoon vanilla extract

7 to 8 tablespoons canned coconut milk or soy creamer

Preheat the oven to 325°F. Line 18 muffin cups (you'll need two 12-cup muffin pans) with paper liners.

For the cupcakes: In a large bowl, sift together the flour, cocoa powder, both starches, cinnamon, cayenne, baking powder, salt, xanthan gum, and baking soda. Whisk to combine.

In a medium bowl, whisk together the agave nectar, milk, oil, applesauce, and vanilla. Add the wet ingredients to the dry ingredients. Using a spatula, thoroughly mix the batter, then let it sit for about 10 minutes to rise.

(continued on page 163)

Pour batter into each liner to about two-thirds full. Bake for 20 to 24 minutes, until a knife or toothpick inserted in the centre of a cupcake comes out clean. Cool completely at room temperature before topping with cinnamon chocolate buttercream.

For the cinnamon chocolate buttercream: Using a stand mixer or hand mixer, cream together the butter and shortening until smooth and fluffy. Slowly add the sugar, mixing well. Add the cocoa powder, cinnamon, vanilla, and then 5 tablespoons coconut milk, adding more as needed to achieve a nice, spreadable consistency. Whip the frosting for several minutes, until fluffy. Use immediately or store in the refrigerator. If refrigerated, bring to room temperature and give it a good turn with a frosting spatula or butter knife before using.

If you are using these to top off a delicious taco party, I suggest grabbing 18 little chili peppers (each about 1 inch tall) to perch on each cupcake. Let only your bravest guests eat the chili.

FRENCH TOAST CUPCAKES

Makes 18 cupcakes

These were originally meant to be a seasonal treat in the fall and winter, but we got too attached to them to stop making them when spring came, and our customers breathed a huge sigh of relief! Cinnamon cake with a nice big swirl of maple frosting on top and a little sprinkle of cinnamon sugar. I don't blame everyone for losing their minds over this one.

1½ cups Bob's Red Mill garbanzo and fava flour

¾ cup potato starch

⅓ cup + 1 tablespoon arrowroot starch

1 tablespoon + ½ teaspoon ground cinnamon

1 tablespoon gluten-free baking powder

1½ teaspoons sea salt

¾ teaspoon xanthan gum

¼ teaspoon baking soda

1 cup agave nectar

¾ cup rice milk

½ cup + 1 tablespoon unsweetened applesauce

½ cup canola oil

2 tablespoons vanilla extract

1 batch maple buttercream frosting (page 235) (2 batches if using a piping bag for big swirls of frosting)

¼ cup organic sugar

Preheat the oven to 325°F. Line 18 muffin cups (you'll need two 12-cup muffin pans) with paper liners.

In a large bowl, sift together the flour, both starches, 1 tablespoon cinnamon, baking powder, salt, xanthan gum, and baking soda. Whisk to combine.

In a medium bowl, whisk together the agave nectar, milk, applesauce, oil, and vanilla. Add the wet ingredients to the dry ingredients. Using a spatula, mix batter well, then let it sit for about 10 minutes to rise.

Pour batter into each liner to about two-thirds full. Bake for 20 to 24 minutes until a knife or toothpick inserted in the centre of a cupcake comes out clean. The cupcakes will be lightly golden on top. Cool completely at room temperature.

Combine the sugar with ½ teaspoon cinnamon. Frost the cupcakes with the maple buttercream. Sprinkle a little cinnamon sugar on top of each frosted cupcake and serve.

SWEET PIES
& TARTS

U sually people assume that vegan and/or gluten-free baking is more difficult than regular baking, and occasionally it can be a challenge, but this is where pastry shines. It becomes easier, if not effortless, to make delicious vegan and gluten-free delights. In traditional pastry, you need to have a light touch so that you don't massage the gluten too much, making the dough tough. With our pastry, you can work it as many times as you like and it will still come out flawless. I know it's obvious to say that it's as easy as pie, but in this case it really is! We've provided you with a bunch of tried-and-true pie recipes, with a few tarts, a crumble, and even something called a grunt thrown in, but feel free to use our pastry recipes to make any and all of your pie desires a reality.

Sweet Pastry...171

Apple Pie...173

Blackberry Peach Pie..175

Blueberry Hand Pies...177

Coconut Cream Pie 179

Butter Tarts 181

Lemon Curd Tarts...185

Blueberry Grunt...187

SWEET PASTRY

Makes enough for one 9-inch single pie shell

This is the good stuff! We are constantly being asked what our pastry secret is, and now the cat's out of the bag. It's officially your recipe too! Use this sweet pastry to make shells for tarts and fruity hand pies, or double the recipe and make a towering apple pie (page 173). The only thing you'll want to avoid is over-flouring the dough if you're rolling it out a few times, as this will dry it up, making it harder to work with and a little less tasty.

1 cup brown rice flour

1 cup Bob's Red Mill garbanzo and fava flour

⅓ cup arrowroot starch

1 tablespoon organic sugar

1 teaspoon xanthan gum

1 teaspoon ground cinnamon

¼ teaspoon sea salt

½ cup Earth Balance Buttery Sticks (1 stick), temperature depends on method used

½ cup Earth Balance Shortening Sticks (1 stick), temperature depends on method used

½ cup cold water

To prepare in a food processor:

In a food processor, combine both flours with the arrowroot starch, sugar, xanthan gum, cinnamon, and salt and pulse a few times to combine.

Cut cold butter and shortening into 2-inch cubes. Add to the flour mixture one cube at a time as you continue to pulse the processor, until the chunks are no longer visible and the mixture takes on a sandy consistency.

Add the water a splash at a time, continuing to pulse the processor. Once all the water is added, process until everything is combined.

Using a spatula, remove the dough from the processor. Divide it in half (for quicker chilling) and, using your hands, flatten each portion into a disc. Wrap in plastic wrap and refrigerate for at least 1 hour, and up to overnight, before using.

To prepare by hand or with a hand mixer:

Bring the butter and shortening to room temperature. In a bowl, cream together the butter and shortening using a potato masher, fork, or hand mixer. In a separate bowl, whisk together all the dry ingredients.

Gradually incorporate the dry ingredients into the creamed butter mixture, mixing with your hands or a fork. Add the cold water a splash at a time until everything is combined.

Divide the dough in half (for quicker chilling), flatten into discs, and wrap in plastic wrap. Refrigerate for at least 90 minutes, and up to overnight, before using.

APPLE PIE

Makes one 9-inch pie

Everyone likes apple pie. Sweet baked cinnamon apple, flaky crust, buttery filling . . . I knew that Bunner's apple pie had a longstanding tradition to live up to, and this recipe can stand crust to crust with the very best.

I like to use Honeycrisp apples because they're firm, tart, and sweet—critical for a great apple pie. That said, you could use any of your favourite pie-making apples. Granny Smith and Pink Lady work well too. Whichever variety you use, I highly recommend organic apples. Apples are one of the heaviest-sprayed fruit crops (along with other soft-skinned fruit like berries and peaches), but you can easily avoid all those harsh chemicals and get the full nutritional benefit of this healthy fruit. Organic apples straight-up taste better, too.

2 batches sweet pastry (page 171)

½ cup Earth Balance Buttery Sticks (1 stick)

3 tablespoons Bob's Red Mill garbanzo and fava flour

½ cup organic sugar

½ cup Sucanat

1½ teaspoons ground cinnamon

8 medium apples, peeled, cored, and sliced ¼ inch thick

Non-dairy milk, for brushing

Prepare the pastry and let chill in the refrigerator for at least 1 hour. Preheat the oven to 375°F.

Remove the dough from the refrigerator. Combine the two discs of one batch and, on a well-floured surface, roll out to a circle about ¼ inch thick and 10 inches in diameter. Transfer to a 9-inch glass pie plate by gently rolling the dough around the rolling pin like a jelly roll, then unrolling it onto the pie plate and lightly pressing it down. If working in a hot or humid environment, refrigerate the pie shell while preparing the apple filling.

In a large saucepan or Dutch oven over medium heat, melt the butter. Whisk in the flour to create a roux. Increase the heat to medium-high, whisking the mixture constantly. When the mixture begins to bubble, whisk in the sugar and Sucanat until fully dissolved, then whisk in the cinnamon.

Reduce the heat to medium-low. Add the apples to the butter mixture in handfuls, stirring to fully coat with the butter. Stir for about 8 to 10 minutes, then pour the apple mixture into the pie shell.

On a well-floured surface, roll out the remaining dough to make a second circle the same size. Using the same method as with the shell, gently place on top of the filling. Trim the overhang and crimp the pastry edges with your fingers or a fork to seal. Slice a few decorative air vents into the top to let out the steam. Lightly brush the pie top with non-dairy milk and sprinkle generously with sugar for a sweet and glossy finish.

Bake for 40 to 45 minutes on the middle oven rack, until the crust is a medium golden brown. Check after 30 minutes. If the top is already a bit too brown, cover with foil; otherwise leave uncovered for the remaining baking time.

Served either warm or cool, this apple pie is especially delicious à la mode with vanilla coconut ice cream.

BLACKBERRY PEACH PIE

Makes one 9-inch pie

There's nothing more satisfying than biting into a ripe juicy organic peach, which is why peach season is one of my favourite times of the year. Peach pies, peach tarts, peach muffins . . . The window is small, so I try to eat as many peaches and peachy treats as I possibly can, to make up for the off-season peach withdrawal.

Not only is this pie a simply delicious combination of sweet and tart, wrapped in a flaky crust, but it looks particularly beautiful once baked, boasting a golden lattice top with the colourful contrast of the peaches and blackberries peeking through.

TIP: If you want to make a straight-up peach pie, simply up the peaches by 2 cups, for a total of 8 cups, and leave out the blackberries.

2 batches sweet pastry (page 171)

6 cups sliced unpeeled peaches (about 8)

2 cups fresh or frozen blackberries

½ cup organic sugar, plus extra for sprinkling

3 tablespoons arrowroot starch

1 teaspoon lemon zest

½ teaspoon ground cinnamon

¼ teaspoon ground nutmeg

2 tablespoons Earth Balance Buttery Sticks, cubed

Non-dairy milk, for brushing

Prepare the pastry and let chill in the refrigerator for at least 1 hour.

Preheat the oven to 375°F.

Remove the dough from the refrigerator. Combine the two discs of one batch and, on a well-floured surface, roll out to a circle about ¼ inch thick and 10 inches in diameter. Transfer by gently rolling the dough around the rolling pin like a jelly roll, then unrolling it onto a 9-inch glass pie plate and lightly pressing it down. Trim the overhang and crimp the pastry edges with your fingers or a fork to seal. If working in a hot or humid environment, refrigerate the pie shell while preparing the filling.

In a large bowl, combine the peaches, blackberries, sugar, arrowroot starch, lemon zest, cinnamon, and nutmeg. Using your hands, mix the ingredients to evenly coat the fruit. Pour the mixture into the pie shell and stud the top with the butter.

On a well-floured surface, roll out the remaining dough to make a second circle the same size. To create a lattice top, cut the dough into eight 1-inch-thick strips. Lay 4 strips horizontally across the pie, then 4 vertically over top, or weave together. Trim the overhang and crimp the pastry edges with your fingers or a fork to seal. Lightly brush the pie top with non-dairy milk and sprinkle generously with sugar for a sweet and glossy finish.

Bake for 40 to 45 minutes on the middle oven rack, until the crust is a medium golden brown. Check the pie after 25 minutes; if the top is already a bit too brown, cover with foil for the remaining baking time.

BLUEBERRY HAND PIES

Makes 8 pies

A hand pie is one of my favourite types of pie because it's so portable and also very cute. At the bakery, we have savoury hand pies, but we call them pockets, and to know them is to love them. These sweet blueberry hand pies would be a welcome addition to any potluck or picnic. Make sure to line the baking sheet with parchment paper—not only can the hand pies get a bit messy as the fruit juices bubble up while baking, but the parchment will keep them from overbrowning on the bottom.

1 batch sweet pastry (page 171)

⅓ cup + 1 tablespoon organic sugar, plus extra for sprinkling

2 tablespoons orange juice or water

1½ tablespoons arrowroot starch

½ teaspoon ground cinnamon

¼ teaspoon sea salt

2 cups fresh or frozen blueberries

Non-dairy milk, for brushing

Prepare the pastry and let chill in the refrigerator for at least 1 hour.

Preheat the oven to 375°F. Line a baking sheet with parchment paper.

In a large bowl, mix together the sugar, orange juice, arrowroot starch, cinnamon, and salt. Add the blueberries, mixing with a spatula or your hands to fully coat the berries.

Divide the dough into eight equal balls. On a floured surface, roll out one ball into a rectangle about 5 × 7 inches and ¼ inch thick. Scoop ¼ cup filling into the centre of the pastry, and fold the pastry over top like a little blanket. Crimp the pastry tightly around the blueberries and trim the excess dough. Using a spatula, gently transfer the hand pie to the prepared baking sheet. Repeat with the remaining pieces of dough and filling.

Slice a couple of decorative air vents into the top to let out the steam.

Lightly brush the pie tops with non-dairy milk and sprinkle with a bit of sugar for a sweet and glossy finish.

Bake for 25 to 30 minutes on the middle oven rack, until golden. Let cool for about 30 minutes before serving.

If you're especially ambitious, drizzle with the lemony glaze used for the Lemon Blackberry Scones (page 33).

COCONUT CREAM PIE

Makes one 9-inch pie

Angela, my roommate in university and one of my best friends on the planet, really loves coconut. She told me this story once about how she was talking to a really hot guy at a bar, and when he asked her what kinds of stuff she liked, all she could squeak out was "Coconut!" Ange is a world traveller these days, but next time she comes home, I'll be using this pie to coerce her to stay a little longer.

TIP: If you will be piping on the whipped cream, or you just want really high fluffy mounds of it, I suggest doubling the amount of whipped cream called for in this recipe—so make 4 batches!

1 batch sweet pastry (page 171)

2 batches coconut whipped cream (page 245)

1 cup unsweetened shredded coconut

½ cup firm silken tofu

3 cups canned coconut milk

⅔ cup organic sugar

¼ teaspoon sea salt

½ cup arrowroot starch

1 teaspoon vanilla extract

Prepare the pastry and whipped cream and let chill in the refrigerator for at least 1 hour.

Preheat the oven to 375°F.

Spread the coconut on an ungreased baking sheet and bake for 10 to 15 minutes, stirring every 5 minutes, until fragrant and golden. Let sit.

Remove the dough from the refrigerator. Combine the two discs and, on a well-floured surface, roll out to a circle about ¼ inch thick and 12 inches in diameter. This will allow room to crimp the edges. Transfer by gently rolling the dough around the rolling pin like a jelly roll, then unrolling it onto a 9-inch glass pie plate and lightly pressing it down. Trim the overhang and crimp the pastry edges with your fingers or a fork to seal. Using a fork, prick the bottom about a dozen times and evenly distribute pie weights or dried beans in the pie shell. Bake for 20 minutes on the middle oven rack, or until the crust is golden brown. Remove from the oven, remove pie weights and let sit.

In a food processor, process the tofu until smooth and creamy. Add 2 cups coconut milk and the sugar and salt. Process until smooth.

In a separate bowl, whisk together the remaining 1 cup coconut milk and arrowroot starch to create a slurry.

In a saucepan over medium-high heat, bring the tofu mixture to a gentle boil. Whisk in the slurry, continuing to whisk until the mixture begins to thicken. Remove from the heat and whisk in the vanilla and ¾ cup toasted coconut.

Pour the mixture into the pie shell and refrigerate for about 4 hours, and up to overnight. Once firmed up, spread or pipe the whipped cream over top and sprinkle with the remaining ¼ cup toasted coconut. Keep cool until ready to serve.

BUTTER TARTS

Makes 12 tarts

Not too many people realize that butter tarts are a Canadian-only classic, eh? Falling into the same category as ketchup chips and Caesars, they're a secret we're happy to keep from the rest of the world if that means there's more for us. If somehow you're unfamiliar with them, they are a flaky little tart with a sticky-sweet, buttery filling that sometimes has raisins and sometimes doesn't. At the bakery, we prefer to use raisins to give it a little extra bite, but you can also substitute walnuts for raisins if you don't have to worry about a nut allergy.

1 batch sweet pastry (page 171)

¾ cup to 1 cup Thompson raisins

⅓ cup + 1 tablespoon canned coconut milk

2 tablespoons arrowroot starch

¼ cup Earth Balance Buttery Sticks (½ stick)

⅓ cup + 1 tablespoon Sucanat

½ cup organic sugar

½ teaspoon vanilla extract

Prepare the pastry and let chill in the refrigerator for at least 1 hour.

Preheat the oven to 375°F. Spray a 12-cup muffin pan with canola oil.

Remove the dough from the refrigerator. Combine the two discs and, on a well-floured surface, roll out to about ¼ inch thick. Using a 3-inch round cookie cutter, cut as many circles as you can. Reroll the dough scraps and cut more circles, until you have 12 circles of dough. Ease a pastry circle into each prepared muffin cup. Drop about 1 tablespoon raisins into each cup and set aside. If the kitchen is hot or humid, place the muffin pan in the refrigerator until the filling is ready.

In a small bowl, whisk together the coconut milk and arrowroot starch to create a slurry.

In a saucepan over medium-high heat, melt the butter and add the Sucanat and sugar, whisking constantly. When completely melted, add the slurry and bring to a gentle boil, continuing to whisk until the mixture thickens. Remove from the heat and stir in the vanilla.

Transfer the hot mixture to a heatproof measuring cup. Carefully pour the liquid into the muffin cups to about three-quarters full; don't overfill.

Bake for 20 minutes on the middle oven rack. Remove from the oven and let sit for 1 hour. Using a butter knife, lift the tarts from the muffin pan and transfer to a resealable container to store in the refrigerator, or to a plate to serve.

Chocol
Glaze

LEMON CURD TARTS

Makes 12 tarts

Lemony desserts serve well all year round: light and breezy for spring and summer, but so in season during the citrus-producing winter months as well. Lemon curd is generally full of egg, so our vegan version has the added bonus of cutting out all the cholesterol from this dessert as well—yippee! Paired with your favourite berries and a spoonful of whipped cream, these tarts will really sing.

1 batch sweet pastry (page 171)

2 batches lemon curd (page 243)

1 cup fresh berries (any combination of
strawberries, blackberries, raspberries,
and blueberries), plus extra for garnish

1 batch coconut whipped cream (page 245)
(optional)

Prepare the pastry and let chill in the refrigerator for at least 1 hour.

Preheat the oven to 375°F. Spray a 12-cup muffin pan with canola spray or, if you like, prepare small tartlet tins.

Remove the dough from the refrigerator. Combine the two discs and, on a well-floured surface, roll out to about ¼ inch thick. Using a 3-inch round cookie cutter, cut as many circles as you can. Reroll the dough scraps and cut more circles, until you have 12 circles of dough. Ease a pastry circle into each prepared muffin cup and prick the bottom of each tart a couple of times with a fork.

Bake the tart shells for 14 to 16 minutes on the middle oven rack, until golden brown (but not too toasty). Remove from the oven and cool completely.

Spoon in the lemon curd, filling the tart shells to just below the edge. Garnish each tart with a dollop of whipped cream (if using) and a few berries.

BLUEBERRY GRUNT

Serves 4 to 6

Blueberry grunt is guaranteed to make you happy—the name alone will make you giggle. Its silly moniker dates back to the early settlers in the Maritimes who named this delicious mixture of blueberries and biscuit-like clouds of dough after the sound the berries made while they simmered in the pot . . . grunt, grunt, grunt!

Now, "down home" in Cape Breton, where Kev's family hails from, mom might ask the kids, "Jeet?" (translation: Did you eat?) and they might reply, "No, jou?" (No, did you?). And if the kids were keeping sweet that day, she just might lay out a pot of blueberry grunt, to which they might excitedly say, "Gway wit ya!" (No way, really!).

Grunts belong to the cobbler, crumble, crisp, and buckle family—a family sometimes so indistinguishable that it feels like you need a PhD to distinguish between them: which one has oats and which does not, which is baked with the crust on the bottom and which on the top. Rest assured, this grunt is quite possibly the simplest dessert in the entire book. Absolutely perfect for a casual weekday dessert treat, maybe not as fancy as you need when the in-laws are in town. Delicious served hot right out of the pot with a nice scoop of coconut ice cream melting on top.

4 cups fresh or frozen blueberries
  (preferably wild)

½ cup + 1 tablespoon organic sugar

½ cup water

1 tablespoon fresh lemon juice

½ teaspoon ground cinnamon

½ teaspoon ground nutmeg

2 cups Bob's Red Mill gluten-free
  all-purpose flour

4 teaspoons gluten-free baking powder

½ teaspoon sea salt

2 tablespoons Earth Balance Buttery Sticks,
  chilled

⅔ cup soy or coconut milk beverage

1 teaspoon vanilla extract

In a large pot over medium-high heat, combine the blueberries, ½ cup sugar, water, lemon juice, cinnamon, and nutmeg. Bring to a gentle boil then reduce heat and let simmer for 20 minutes.

Meanwhile, in a medium bowl, whisk together the flour, baking powder, salt, and the remaining 1 tablespoon sugar. Cut in the chilled butter with a knife or pastry blender until the mixture takes on a sandy consistency. Add the milk and vanilla and mix with a wooden spoon or fork until a soft dough is formed.

Using your hands, loosely form 2½-inch-wide biscuit shapes out of the dough and drop these onto the blueberry sauce, spacing them as evenly as possible so that they cover as much of the sauce's surface as possible. Cover the pot and cook over medium-low heat for 15 minutes without lifting the lid. After 15 minutes, take a peek inside—the biscuits should be a toasty light brown on top. If they aren't, replace the lid and cook for another 3 to 5 minutes before checking again.

Serve hot, dished into bowls with a nice scoop of coconut vanilla ice cream.

HOLIDAY

The winter holidays bring with them a sense of warm and often romantic nostalgia. We love to see the snow falling on a crisp, calm night, to smell the fresh pine as we pick out a Christmas tree, to gather up our family and see all the faces of the people we love at one time. Not to mention all the eating we get to do! That's why the holiday chapter is always my favourite section of any baking book. With a distinct array of warming spices in buttery baked goods, traditional holiday baking is a unique and decadent taste sensation—but one that can be torture if you're left wanting for vegan and gluten-free treats. No longer! You'll be back in the thick of your cookie-making tradition with our banana rum cookies, delicious shortbread, and gingerbread people. We've also got pies, crisps, and even a cheesecake to indulge in. And yes, you'll find our much-sought-after stuffing recipe here too. By all means, though, don't wait for the cold weather to start making these treats. Who says you can't reminisce with a little pumpkin pie in July?

Maple Plum Pie...193

Pumpkin Pie...195

Apple Crisp..197

Cranberry Pear Crisp 199

Pumpkin Cheesecake..201

Gingerbread Cookies 203

Spiced Banana Rum Cookies..205

Shortbread Cookies 207

Sugar Cookies...209

Rugelach 211

Peppermint Bark 213

Savoury Holiday Stuffing...215

MAPLE PLUM PIE

Makes one 9-inch pie

For our first Thanksgiving at the bakery, I wanted to create something that was unique and sounded delicious, an unusual pie that might rival the more traditional apple or pumpkin. Lo and behold, this pie was more popular than our classic apple pie! We take fresh red plums and use the darkest grade of maple syrup available to give this pie a deliciously fruity, all-Canadian appeal.

2 batches sweet pastry (page 171)

4 cups pitted and sliced red- or purple-skinned plums

⅓ cup organic sugar

¼ cup Bob's Red Mill gluten-free all-purpose flour

1 teaspoon ground cinnamon

¼ teaspoon ground nutmeg

¼ teaspoon sea salt

¼ cup dark maple syrup

1 teaspoon maple extract (optional)

Rice milk, for brushing

Prepare the pastry and let chill in the refrigerator for at least 1 hour.

Preheat the oven to 375°F.

In a large bowl, toss together the plums, sugar, flour, cinnamon, nutmeg, and salt. Add the maple syrup and maple extract (if using) and toss again to coat the fruit.

Remove the dough from the refrigerator. Combine the two discs of one batch and, on a well-floured surface, roll out to a circle about ¼ inch thick and 10 inches in diameter. Transfer to a 9-inch glass pie plate by gently rolling the dough around the rolling pin like a jelly roll, then unrolling it onto the pie plate and lightly pressing it down.

Fill the pie shell with the plum mixture, spreading it out evenly.

On a well-floured surface, roll out the remaining dough to make a second circle the same size. Using the same method as with the shell, lay it on top of the filling. Trim the overhang and crimp the pastry edges with your fingers or a fork to seal.

Using a sharp knife, make a few decorative air vents in the top. Lightly brush with milk and sprinkle generously with sugar so that it bakes up with a sweet and golden gloss. Bake for 45 minutes, or until the crust is medium golden brown. Check after 25 minutes. If the top is already a bit too brown, cover with foil; otherwise leave un-covered for the remaining baking time.

Let cool to room temperature before serving.

PUMPKIN PIE

Makes one 9-inch pie

Pumpkin pie is one of those treats that herald the end of summer and the beginning of fall. Even by the end of August we have diehard pumpkin fans begging us to tell them when we'll start making this classic. We usually wait until Thanksgiving weekend to kick off pumpkin pie season, and we'll make hundreds of them in the span of three days. Be sure to use canned pumpkin (preferably organic) and not pumpkin pie filling, which is presweetened and spiced. You can also roast and purée the pumpkin yourself if you're especially ambitious.

1 batch sweet pastry (page 171)

2¼ cups pure pumpkin purée

⅓ cup + 1 tablespoon dark maple syrup

⅓ cup + 1 tablespoon canned coconut milk

1½ tablespoons arrowroot starch

1 tablespoon canola oil

1 teaspoon ground cinnamon

1 teaspoon ground ginger

¾ teaspoon agar-agar

½ teaspoon sea salt

¼ teaspoon ground nutmeg

Prepare the pastry and let chill in the refrigerator for at least 1 hour.

Preheat the oven to 375°F.

Remove the dough from the refrigerator. Combine the two discs and, on a well-floured surface, roll out to a circle about ¼ inch thick and 10 inches in diameter. Transfer to a 9-inch glass pie plate by gently rolling the dough around the rolling pin like a jelly roll, then unrolling it onto the pie plate and lightly pressing it down. Trim the overhang and crimp the pastry edges with your fingers or a fork to seal.

In a blender or large bowl, combine the pumpkin purée, maple syrup, coconut milk, arrowroot starch, oil, cinnamon, ginger, agar-agar, salt, and nutmeg. Blend or whisk until smooth.

Pour the filling into the pie shell, using a spatula to smooth out the top. Bake for 45 minutes.

Let cool for about 30 minutes before refrigerating, and let set for at least 4 hours, and up to overnight, before slicing. Serve with a little coconut whipped cream (page 245) for a real palate pleaser.

APPLE CRISP

Makes one 8-inch dish

This recipe is one of the easiest things you could whip up. The most difficult part is peeling the apples! Make sure to get nice firm, tart ones like Granny Smith, Honeycrisp, or Pink Lady. Perfect for the holidays or at a fall brunch, this apple crisp may be in the holiday chapter but don't hesitate to make it all year round.

At the bakery, we made it once with organic coconut sugar to switch it up a bit. Although this recipe calls for organic sugar and Sucanat, you can definitely swap in organic coconut sugar or organic brown sugar for the Sucanat.

5 cups peeled, cored, and sliced apples (about 4 apples)

½ cup organic sugar

½ cup + 1½ teaspoons Bob's Red Mill gluten-free all-purpose flour

½ teaspoon ground cinnamon

¼ cup water

½ cup gluten-free rolled oats

½ cup Sucanat

⅛ teaspoon gluten-free baking powder

⅛ teaspoon baking soda

¼ cup melted coconut oil

Preheat the oven to 350°F. Have an ovenproof dish ready—any dish with a 6-cup capacity will work well.

In a large bowl, toss the apples with the sugar, 1½ teaspoons flour, and cinnamon until well coated. Add the water and toss until the apples are consistently coated. Pour the apples into the baking dish, spreading them out evenly.

In a medium bowl, mix together the oats, the remaining ½ cup flour, Sucanat, baking powder, and baking soda. Add the oil and mix until it forms a loose dough. Using your hands, spread the mixture evenly on top of the apples.

Bake for 45 minutes or until the apples are broken down and can be pierced easily with a fork (and your kitchen smells fantastic).

Serve warm with a nice scoop of vanilla coconut milk ice cream.

CRANBERRY PEAR CRISP

Makes one 8-inch crisp

Pears and cranberries together make such a wintery, delicious, and unexpected combination. Bosc pears work especially well, since they hold their shape a bit better when baking than the other pear varieties but, truly, any pear would suffice. According to our bakery manager, Amelia, not only does this make a lovely Christmas dessert, it also makes for a very tummy-warming breakfast on Christmas morning (or any winter morning that needs an extra pick-me-up, for that matter).

5 cups unpeeled, cored, and chopped pears (about 4 pears cut into 1-inch cubes)

1 cup fresh or frozen cranberries

1 cup organic sugar

½ cup + 2 tablespoons Bob's Red Mill gluten-free all-purpose flour

¼ teaspoon ground cinnamon

¼ teaspoon ground nutmeg

½ cup gluten-free rolled oats

⅛ teaspoon gluten-free baking powder

⅛ teaspoon baking soda

¼ cup melted coconut oil

Preheat the oven to 350°F. Have an 8-inch glass baking dish ready.

Place the pears and cranberries in a large bowl. Add ½ cup sugar, 2 tablespoons flour, cinnamon, and nutmeg. Toss until the fruit is well coated. Pour the fruit mixture into the baking dish.

In the same bowl, add the oats, the remaining ½ cup flour, the remaining ½ cup sugar, baking powder, and baking soda. Whisk to combine. Add the oil and mix until well combined. Using your hands, crumble the mixture evenly over top of the fruit.

Bake for 40 to 45 minutes, until the topping is golden brown and you can see the filling bubbling up.

Let cool for about 10 minutes before serving with a nice scoop of non-dairy ice cream.

PUMPKIN CHEESECAKE

Makes one 8-inch cake

A magical hybrid of pumpkin pie and cheesecake, this delicious dessert is so creamy and yummy, your guests will be thoroughly spellbound. Like our Chocolate Cheesecake (page 145), Bunner's Pumpkin Cheesecake tastes delightfully sinful, and the addition of the chocolate crust and a ganache spread on top sends this extraordinary dessert right over the edge of indulgence. Such a refreshing twist on an old holiday fave.

1½ cups double chocolate-chip cookie crumbs (use your favourite brand of cookies or our recipe, page 93)

⅓ cup melted coconut oil

2 8-oz tubs Tofutti non-hydrogenated vegan cream cheese

1 15-oz can pure pumpkin purée

½ cup Sucanat

½ cup organic sugar

3 tablespoons arrowroot starch

1 teaspoon ground cinnamon

½ teaspoon ground ginger

¼ teaspoon ground nutmeg

1 batch chocolate ganache (page 241)

Preheat the oven to 350°F. Spray an 8-inch springform pan with canola oil.

In a large bowl, combine the cookie crumbs with the oil. Mix with a fork until the crumb mixture holds its shape when squeezed together. Using your hands, press the crumb mixture evenly over the base of the springform pan to create the crust.

In a food processor, process the cream cheese until completely smooth, like a thick pudding. Add the pumpkin purée and process until combined. Add the Sucanat, sugar, arrowroot starch, cinnamon, ginger, and nutmeg and process again, stopping occasionally to scrape down the sides of the work bowl, until well combined, thick, and creamy.

Pour the pumpkin filling onto the prepared crust, using a spatula to scrape out all the pumpkin goodness from the bowl, and smooth the top neatly and evenly.

Bake for 45 minutes, then turn off the oven and let the cake rest in the hot oven for another 30 minutes. Let cool before placing in the refrigerator to set for 3 hours, and up to overnight.

To remove the cake from the pan, run a sharp knife around the edge before releasing the sides of the springform pan.

Before serving, spread a layer of ganache up to ¼ inch thick over top of the cake. Let set in the refrigerator for 20 minutes. Then slice and serve.

GINGERBREAD COOKIES

Makes 12 to 18 cookies

These cookies are adapted from one of my favourite old recipes. We made them vegan, gluten-free, and soy-free, and the results are so totally delicious, they are by far one of our most popular holiday items. So much so that people ask for them all year round.

Now, you can cut these into people shapes or Christmassy shapes, or you can buy a cookie-cutter kit to make your own gingerbread houses. These cookies work well for anything, but just be sure to increase the baking time by a few minutes if you're baking anything larger than your average cookie, or to decrease it a little if you're using a very delicate cookie-cutter shape.

The maple nutmeg glaze (page 35) works well for decoration, and the vanilla dip we use for our donuts (page 119) is ideal for sticking your gingerbread home together.

2 cups Bob's Red Mill gluten-free all-purpose flour

1½ teaspoons ground ginger

½ teaspoon ground cinnamon

½ teaspoon ground nutmeg

½ teaspoon gluten-free baking powder

½ teaspoon baking soda

½ teaspoon xanthan gum

½ teaspoon sea salt

¾ cup organic sugar

⅓ cup canola oil

¼ cup organic blackstrap molasses

¼ cup rice milk

In a large bowl, sift together the flour, ginger, cinnamon, nutmeg, baking powder, baking soda, xanthan gum, and salt. Whisk to combine.

In a medium bowl, whisk together the sugar, oil, molasses, and milk. Add the wet ingredients to the dry ingredients. Using a spatula or a stand mixer with the paddle attachment, combine to form a soft dough. Divide the dough into two balls and flatten into discs. Wrap in plastic wrap and place in the refrigerator for about 1 hour.

Preheat the oven to 350°F. Line two baking sheets with parchment paper.

On a floured work surface, roll out the dough to about ¼ inch thick. Cut out shapes with cookie cutters, rerolling any scraps of dough and cutting out more shapes until the dough is used up. Place on the prepared baking sheets, spacing about 1 inch apart.

Bake for 8 to 10 minutes, until light brown and slightly puffy. Let cool on the baking sheets for 10 minutes before transferring to a cooling rack.

Cool completely before decorating or eating.

SPICED BANANA RUM COOKIES

Makes 24 small cookies

Spiced-up bananas and rum are an amazing flavour combination that really puts you in the festive mood. We started on the path toward making rum balls but at some point turned left instead of right and wound up arriving at this amazingly buttery, fluffy cookie. If you're the type to really get into the decorating spirit, add your very own personal touch by topping with the optional frosting.

TIP: Be sure to use dark rum, and not spiced rum, which may contain a few pesky gluten-containing spices. You can also use rum extract if you have it on hand.

1¾ cups Bob's Red Mill gluten-free
    all-purpose flour

1½ teaspoons gluten-free baking powder

½ teaspoon xanthan gum

½ teaspoon sea salt

½ teaspoon ground cinnamon

½ teaspoon ground nutmeg

¼ teaspoon baking soda

½ cup mashed ripe banana (1 to 2 freckled
    bananas)

¼ cup canola oil

¾ cup organic sugar

2 tablespoons dark rum

1 tablespoon organic blackstrap molasses

1½ teaspoons vanilla extract

Frosting (Optional)

2 tablespoons Earth Balance Buttery Sticks,
    at room temperature

2 cups organic powdered sugar, plus extra as
    needed

2 tablespoons soy or coconut milk beverage,
    plus extra as needed

2 tablespoons dark rum

Coloured sugar, shredded toasted coconut,
    or freshly grated nutmeg, for decoration

Preheat the oven to 350°F. Line two baking sheets with parchment paper.

In a medium bowl, sift together the flour, baking powder, xanthan gum, salt, cinnamon, nutmeg, and baking soda. Whisk to combine.

In a small bowl, thoroughly whisk the banana with the oil. Whisk in the sugar, rum, molasses, and vanilla. Pour the wet ingredients into the dry ingredients and mix well using a spatula.

With clean hands, roll lumps of cookie dough into golf-ball-size pieces. Do not flatten. Place each ball on the prepared baking sheets about 2 inches apart.

Bake for 10 minutes, or until golden brown and puffy. Cool for 20 minutes before transferring to a cooling rack.

For the frosting (if using): Cream the butter using a hand mixer or fork. Slowly add the sugar until the mixture is quite stiff. Add the milk and rum, mixing quickly. Add more sugar or milk as needed for a somewhat firm consistency. Drizzle the frosting on the cookies and decorate using coloured sugar, coconut, or nutmeg. Let frosting set before serving.

SHORTBREAD COOKIES

Makes 20 cookies

Okay, everyone, you can start rejoicing now: melt-in-your-mouth shortbreads are here again! Over the years, I've searched fruitlessly for a shortbread that reminded me of the delicious little biscuits of my childhood. My search is over because this cookie is pure, unadulterated shortbread goodness, just like its butter-and-wheat-laden predecessors. You may choose to doll it up with flavoured extracts, but I love it as is, just as plain Jane as the day it was baked. If you want to dress it up for the winter holidays, carefully dip half of each cookie into melted chocolate and sprinkle with a touch of candied orange peel. Or go full-on classic and garnish with red or green maraschino cherries.

1 cup Earth Balance Buttery Sticks (2 sticks), at room temperature

½ cup organic powdered sugar

1½ cups Bob's Red Mill gluten-free all-purpose flour

¼ cup arrowroot starch

¼ teaspoon xanthan gum

¼ teaspoon sea salt

Preheat the oven to 375°F. Line two baking sheets with parchment paper.

In a large bowl, cream together the butter and sugar.

In a medium bowl, sift together the flour, arrowroot starch, xanthan gum, and salt. Add the dry ingredients to the creamed butter and, using a spatula, mix until combined.

With clean hands, form the dough into tablespoon-size balls and place on the prepared baking sheets. Press down to slightly flatten the cookies, being mindful to keep them spaced about 2 inches apart.

Bake until the tops of the cookies are matte and have just a hint of golden colour, about 10 minutes. Overbaking by even a minute or two can burn the bottoms, so keep a close eye on them.

Let cool on the baking sheets for 5 minutes before transferring to a cooling rack to cool completely.

TIP: If garnishing with maraschino cherries, press a piece into the centre of each cookie before baking.

SUGAR COOKIES

Makes 18 cookies

The jingle of sleigh bells breaks the silence of a quiet Christmas Eve. A crash is heard at the base of the chimney and, through a puff of soot, out walks jolly old St. Nick. He looks to the tree and sees it strung with an impressive popcorn garland. Pleased, he moves toward the Christmas tree, but something is amiss. His eyes dart left, then right, but where is his plate of festive sugar cookies? And then the man in red sees him: Dad, curled up on the couch in his housecoat, his collection of Rush records scattered around the living room, a few sugary crumbs peppering his moustache. Looks like Dad might have some 'splainin' to do . . .

Sugar cookies aren't just for Santa anymore. Not only are they fun to decorate, but they can be cut into pretty much any shape imaginable. Frost a spooky jack-o'-lantern at Halloween or a bunny at Easter, pick up a dinosaur cookie cutter for nibbles during the class trip to the museum, or spread on some delightful bubble-gum-pink buttercream with sprinkles for a little retro birthday fun. They're the all-purpose special occasion cookie, and when it comes to decorating, you won't have any trouble recruiting your family and friends to get the job done. (Note: Dad is not invited.)

1 cup Earth Balance Buttery Sticks (2 sticks)	¾ teaspoon xanthan gum
1 cup organic sugar	¼ teaspoon sea salt
¾ cup vanilla coconut yogurt	1 batch donut glaze (page 237) (optional)
2 teaspoons vanilla extract	1 batch vanilla buttercream frosting (page 225)
3½ cups Bob's Red Mill gluten-free all-purpose flour	(optional)
	Sprinkles, for decorating (optional)

In a large bowl using a spatula or fork, cream together the butter and sugar. Add the yogurt and vanilla and mix until well combined.

In a medium bowl, sift together the flour, xanthan gum, and salt. Add to the wet ingredients and mix well using a spatula until a soft dough is formed. Divide the dough in half and shape into two discs. Cover in plastic wrap and refrigerate for at least 1 hour.

Preheat the oven to 375°F. Line two baking sheets with parchment paper.

On a well-floured surface, roll out one disc to about ½ inch thick. Using a 2½-inch cookie cutter, cut into desired shape and transfer to the prepared baking sheets, spacing about 1 inch apart.

Bake for 10 to 12 minutes, until a peek under the bottom of a cookie shows a light golden colour.

Cool on the baking sheets for 5 minutes before transferring to a cooling rack to cool completely.

If desired, decorate with the donut glaze tinted with a few drops of food colouring or beet juice, or with a layer of vanilla buttercream with sprinkles scattered on top. Serve often, and with tea (or milk, as your Santa requests).

RUGELACH

Makes 18 to 24 cookies

While testing the recipes for this book, I could always tell when I really liked one by my total inability to stop eating it. These little monsters wouldn't stop beckoning me from the kitchen, coercing me back time and again with their flaky pastry and sweet apricot and raisin filling. Traditionally Jewish, rugelach can be stuffed with pretty much anything. I chose apricot jam and Thompson raisins, but you can use chopped walnuts, pistachios, mini chocolate chips, even cake or cookie crumbs left over from your baking adventures. There are about 1001 variations online, so use your little fingers to Google up your own crazy concoction. Beteavon! (That's Hebrew for bon appetit, which is French for "hands off my treat!")

1 8-oz tub Tofutti non-hydrogenated vegan cream cheese

1 cup Earth Balance Buttery Sticks (2 sticks)

¼ cup organic sugar

1 teaspoon vanilla extract

¼ teaspoon xanthan gum

¼ teaspoon sea salt

2 cups Bob's Red Mill gluten-free all-purpose flour

1½ teaspoons ground cinnamon

½ cup apricot jam

¾ cup Thompson raisins, left whole or coarsely chopped

In a large bowl, cream together the cream cheese and butter using a hand mixer or stand mixer. Add the sugar, vanilla, xanthan gum, and salt, mixing thoroughly to combine. Slowly sift in the flour and cinnamon, mixing well. You can also use your hands to mix the dough, but if you do, start with a fork first, using your hands when the crumbs start to come together.

Divide the dough into three portions and shape each into a disc. Wrap in plastic wrap and refrigerate for at least 1 hour.

Preheat the oven to 350°F. Line two baking sheets with parchment paper.

On a floured work surface, roll out one disc of dough to form a large circle about ⅛ inch thick. Using a butter knife, cut the circle into 6 or 8 triangular wedges (like slicing a pie), depending on the desired cookie size.

Spread about 2½ tablespoons jam over the top, all the way to the edges. Sprinkle ¼ cup raisins over top. Starting from the wide edge of each triangle, roll the dough toward the centre, forming a croissant-shaped roll. Transfer to the prepared baking sheet, and repeat with remaining dough wedges, placing about ½ inch apart. Repeat process with the remaining two discs of dough.

Bake for 20 minutes for smaller cookies (8 slices per disc, or 24 cookies total), and 24 minutes for larger cookies (6 slices per disc, or 18 cookies total), or until the bottoms are a warm, golden colour (lift the cookies with a fork or spatula to check).

PEPPERMINT BARK

Strips of the outermost layer of the peppermint tree? No. The sound a dog makes after he's just brushed his teeth? Nope! What we're talking about is the timeless combination of chocolate and peppermint, and let me assure you, making this recipe is so delicious and simple, it's almost like cheating.

I have been making this holiday treat for as long as I can remember, and continue to have requests for it every year. If you're in a last-minute pickle about what to bring to the next holiday potluck, or if you want a thoughtful handmade gift for your Secret Santa, this one's for you.

While I was in university (and my pocketbook was extremely lean), I still tried to buy the very best chocolate I could find for my bark. It's the ingredient this recipe hinges on. If you can't find dairy-free white chocolate, use semi-sweet chocolate in its place. If you are using chocolate chips instead of chopped chocolate, you'll need about 2⅔ cups of each.

18 ounces vegan bittersweet chocolate, chopped

½ teaspoon peppermint oil

18 ounces vegan white chocolate, chopped

¾ cup crushed gluten-free candy canes

Line an 11- × 17-inch baking sheet with parchment paper.

Using a double boiler over medium heat, melt the bittersweet chocolate. (If you don't have a double boiler, use a heatproof measuring cup placed in a saucepan filled with 1 to 2 inches of water.) Ensure you don't get any water in the chocolate or it will seize up and turn chunky. Once the chocolate is melted and silky, stir in ¼ teaspoon peppermint oil. Pour the melted chocolate onto the prepared baking sheet and refrigerate for 1 hour, or until firm.

Melt the white chocolate using the same method. Once melted, stir in the remaining ¼ teaspoon peppermint oil and the candy canes. Spread the white chocolate mixture over the chilled bittersweet chocolate and refrigerate until completely firm, at least 4 hours or even overnight.

To serve, break into bite-size shards. Store layered on parchment paper in an airtight container in the refrigerator.

SAVOURY HOLIDAY STUFFING

Serves 4

For me, this is a traditional stuffing, but it occurred to me that "traditional stuffing" is completely subjective. Maybe you call it "dressing," or make it with cornbread or mushrooms or sausages or all sorts of crazy things. Essentially, this is a pretty basic stuffing that you can doll up to your heart's desire. My mom taught me this during the first vegan Christmas we celebrated together. I have outlined the recipe below, but I expect you to taste-test and add a little of this and a little of that until it's spot-on to your liking.

6 cups 1-inch gluten-free stale bread cubes*

¼ cup Earth Balance Buttery Sticks (½ stick)

½ medium yellow onion, minced

½ cup minced carrot

1 stalk celery, minced

2 teaspoons dried thyme

2 teaspoons dried rubbed sage

½ cup gluten-free vegetable stock

Sea salt

Preheat the oven to 375°F. Have ready a 9-inch glass baking dish or small casserole dish.

Place the bread cubes in a large bowl.

In a large saucepan over medium heat, melt the butter. Add the onions and cook for about 10 minutes, then add the carrot, celery, thyme, and sage. Sauté for 10 minutes, stirring occasionally.

Using a wooden spoon, toss the bread with the mixture to evenly coat. Add the stock, then salt to taste.

Transfer the stuffing to the baking dish and cover with foil. Bake for 30 minutes, then remove the foil and bake for another 5 to 15 minutes, until the topping is crisped to your liking.

*To make "stale" bread cubes, cut a fresh loaf of bread into ½-inch pieces. Spread evenly over a non-greased baking sheet and bake in a 200°F oven for 20 minutes. Let cool before using.

FROSTINGS & TOPPINGS

W hat does the perfect shade of lipstick (to match your new red dress) have in common with an ironic moustache on a hipster (drinking an espresso)? Why, they're both the icing on the cake, of course! It's an expression we use when we add that perfect *je ne sais quoi*, that indescribable but oh-so-desirable finishing touch to a masterpiece. The last, bold stroke of colour by the master painter that says *"Voilà!"*

Well, in the context of this book, that last, bold stroke is a creamy, buttery frosting; a to-die-for decadent caramel sauce; a dollop of fluffy, cool coconut whipped cream; or a sassy, lip-puckering lemon curd. The palette knife is your brush, these frostings and toppings are your paints, and the delicious cakes, cupcakes, and pastries you've worked to create are your canvas. Be. The. Master.

How to Frost a Cake 220
Vanilla Buttercream Frosting... 225
Chocolate Buttercream Frosting.. 227
Cream Cheese Frosting 229
Lemon Buttercream Frosting... 233
Maple Buttercream Frosting 235
Donut Glaze... 237
Caramel Sauce... 239
Chocolate Ganache... 241
Lemon Curd 243
Coconut Whipped Cream.. 245

How to Frost a Cake

1. Begin with two level rounds of cake that have been chilled for at least 2 hours, and make sure the frosting is a spreadable consistency. If it's too firm, it will make frosting the cake a real pain. You can loosen it up by letting it come to room temperature or by turning it vigorously a few times with a knife or frosting spatula until it's the consistency you're looking for.

2. Place one cake round on a plate or serving platter. Scoop on a heaping cup of frosting. Using a butter knife (or, better, a frosting spatula), smooth down the frosting to the desired thickness for between the two layers. With the excess frosting, frost the sides of this bottom layer.

3. Place the second layer on top of the first, making sure that it is perfectly centred on the bottom layer.

4. Scoop on another cup of frosting and repeat the process, spreading it on as thick as you like.

5. Frost the sides of the top layer, blending into the frosting on the bottom layer.

6. Go over the cake with a frosting spatula or knife a few times to create a smoother texture.

7. For a cleaner and more pro-looking cake, grab a piping bag and pipe on a bottom and a top border. We've used a star tip here, but you can use any tip you like. These can be as simple as you like and they'll still look great.

8. Use another piping bag, this time with a round tip, to write a cute message on top of the cake. Finish decorating with any sprinkles or candles you wish to use, and serve.

VANILLA BUTTERCREAM FROSTING

Makes 4 cups

Our amazing frosting is the cornerstone of the bakery's reputation, and it often leaves people wondering how we pull off such a decadent buttercream sans butter. Soft, sweet, creamy, and not at all grainy. The trick to an ultimately smooth texture is to use powdered sugar and sift it by hand. In fact, at the bakery, we hand-sift more than 100 pounds of icing sugar in an average week. It makes for some strong arms, not to mention a lot of frosting!

½ cup Earth Balance Buttery Sticks (1 stick), at room temperature

½ cup Earth Balance Shortening Sticks (1 stick), at room temperature

3½ cups organic powdered sugar, sifted

1 to 2 teaspoons vanilla extract

3 to 5 tablespoons canned coconut milk or soy creamer

Using a stand mixer or hand mixer, cream together the butter and shortening until completely smooth and fluffy. Slowly add the sugar, mixing well. Stir in the vanilla and then 3 tablespoons coconut milk, adding milk as needed to achieve a nice, spreadable consistency.

Whip the frosting for several minutes, until fluffy. Use immediately or store in the refrigerator. If refrigerated, bring to room temperature and give it a good turn with a frosting spatula or butter knife before spreading this luscious frosting on your awaiting treats.

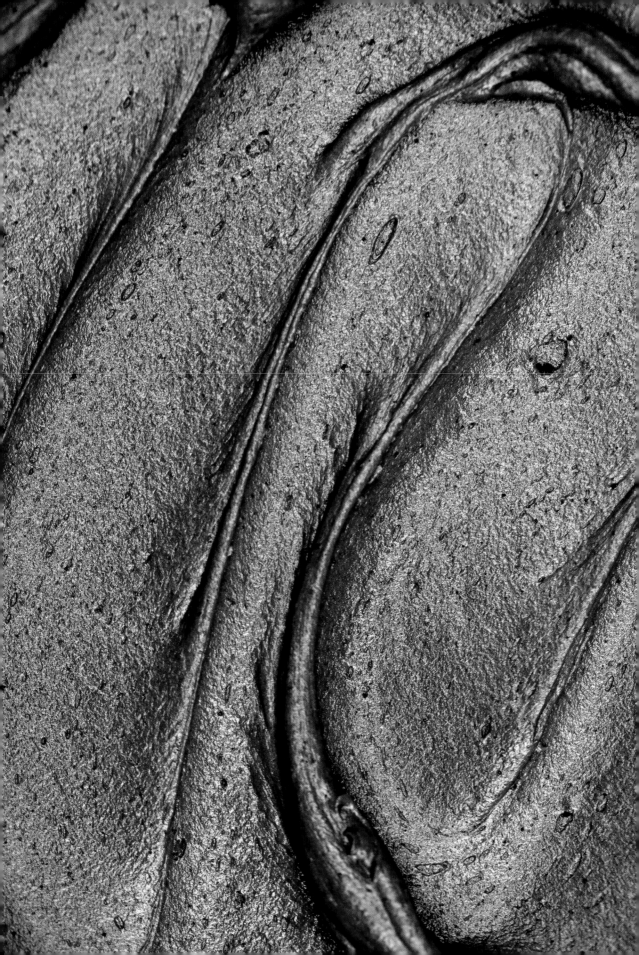

CHOCOLATE BUTTERCREAM FROSTING

Makes 4 cups

Chocolate buttercream is my favourite frosting, and you can often find me slathering it on everything at the bakery before having a little nibble. The creamy, chocolaty rich texture is to die for and perfectly complements the decadent Birthday Cake (page 129) and our renowned Chocolate Cupcakes (page 153).

½ cup Earth Balance Buttery Sticks (1 stick), at room temperature

½ cup Earth Balance Shortening Sticks (1 stick), at room temperature

3½ cups organic powdered sugar, sifted

¾ cup unsweetened cocoa powder, sifted

1 teaspoon vanilla extract

5 to 7 tablespoons canned coconut milk or soy creamer

Using a stand mixer or hand mixer, cream together the butter and shortening until smooth and fluffy.

Slowly add the sugar, mixing well. Add the cocoa powder, vanilla, and then 5 tablespoons coconut milk, adding more as needed to achieve a nice, spreadable consistency.

Whip the frosting for several minutes, until fluffy. Use immediately or store in the refrigerator. If refrigerated, bring to room temperature and give it a good turn with a frosting spatula or butter knife before using.

CREAM CHEESE FROSTING

Makes about 2 cups

This is just the most scrumptious frosting, so please feel free to spread it on everything. It is particularly good with Red Velvet Cake (page 133), but you can also swap this in on the Strawberry Cake (page 137), or even the Pound Cake (page 143) if you want to add a little rich, creamy pizzazz.

½ cup Earth Balance Buttery Sticks (1 stick), at room temperature

½ cup Tofutti non-hydrogenated vegan cream cheese

3½ cups organic powdered sugar, sifted

1 teaspoon vanilla extract

2 to 3 tablespoons canned coconut milk or soy creamer

Using a stand mixer or hand mixer, cream together the butter and cream cheese until smooth and fluffy.

Slowly add the sugar, mixing well. Add the vanilla and then 2 tablespoons coconut milk, adding more as needed to achieve a nice, spreadable consistency.

Whip the frosting for several minutes, until fluffy. Use immediately or store in the refrigerator. If refrigerated, bring to room temperature and give it a good turn with a frosting spatula or butter knife before using.

LEMON BUTTERCREAM FROSTING

Makes 4 cups

This lemon frosting pairs perfectly with Lemon Cupcakes (page 157), but feel free to spread it on a full-size cake as well—specifically the Birthday Cake (page 129), the Strawberry Cake (page 137), or, for a unique twist, the rich Chocolate Cake (page 131).

½ cup Earth Balance Buttery Sticks (1 stick), at room temperature

½ cup Earth Balance Shortening Sticks (1 stick), at room temperature

3½ cups organic powdered sugar, sifted

2 teaspoons lemon extract

1 teaspoon vanilla extract

3 to 5 tablespoons canned coconut milk or soy creamer

Using a stand mixer or hand mixer, cream together the butter and shortening until smooth and fluffy.

Slowly add the sugar, mixing well. Add the vanilla and lemon extract, and then 3 tablespoons coconut milk, adding more as needed to achieve a nice, spreadable consistency.

Whip the frosting for several minutes, until fluffy. Use immediately or store in the refrigerator. If refrigerated, bring to room temperature and give it a good turn with a frosting spatula or butter knife before using.

MAPLE BUTTERCREAM FROSTING

Makes 4 cups

The crescendo of our French Toast Cupcake (page 165)! You can also pair this frosting with Ashley's Delight Cake (page 139) for an amazing cake combo. The maple syrup is optional, though it does add a real maple kick to the frosting. Use a dark amber maple syrup for the most potent flavour.

½ cup Earth Balance Buttery Sticks (1 stick), at room temperature

½ cup Earth Balance Shortening Sticks (1 stick), at room temperature

3½ cups organic powdered sugar, sifted

1 teaspoon vanilla extract

1 teaspoon maple extract (optional)

3 to 5 tablespoons dark maple syrup

Using a stand mixer or hand mixer, cream together the butter and shortening until smooth and fluffy.

Slowly add the sugar, mixing well. Add the vanilla, maple extract (if using), and then 3 tablespoons maple syrup, adding more as needed to achieve a nice, spreadable consistency.

Whip the frosting for several minutes, until fluffy. Use immediately or store in the refrigerator. If refrigerated, bring to room temperature and give it a good turn with a frosting spatula or butter knife before using.

DONUT GLAZE

Makes 1 cup

It took me a long time to perfect this glaze. I was after that ideal texture: not so dry that it's like protective armour, and not so wet that it absorbs right into the donut. This glaze is just right—it's the kind that crinkles when you touch it. It's a total standout on a donut, but you can use it on lots of other goodies. Drizzling it over the Lemon Blackberry Scones (page 33) is just one fabulous idea.

5 tablespoons Earth Balance Buttery Sticks

2 cups organic powdered sugar, sifted

¼ cup warm water

1½ tablespoons vanilla extract

In a saucepan over medium heat, melt the butter. Add the sugar, water, and vanilla and stir until the mixture is smooth. Remove from the heat and use the glaze immediately. Reheat if it becomes too stiff.

CARAMEL SAUCE

Makes 1½ cups

This caramel sauce is completely delicious and convincing, but it's difficult to have in the refrigerator because you'll want to keep sneaking spoonfuls! It's the main event in our Caramel Cupcakes (page 159), but feel free to get creative. Drizzle over cheesecakes, tarts, donuts—the sky's the limit!

1 cup canned coconut milk

1 tablespoon + 1 teaspoon arrowroot starch

½ cup brown rice syrup

¼ cup organic sugar

¼ cup Sucanat

2 tablespoons Earth Balance Buttery Sticks

2 teaspoons vanilla extract

⅛ teaspoon sea salt

In a small bowl, whisk together ¼ cup coconut milk and the arrowroot starch to create a slurry.

In a medium saucepan over medium-high heat, combine the remaining ¾ cup coconut milk, brown rice syrup, sugar, and Sucanat. Bring to a gentle boil, whisking often. Let the mixture bubble away for about 10 seconds, then whisk in the butter. Decrease the heat to low and let simmer for about 10 minutes, whisking often. Whisk in the slurry. Let simmer, whisking constantly, until the sauce begins to coat the whisk (it will not be very thick). Don't let the sauce boil too hard or it will become stretchy and gel-like. Remove from the heat and stir in the vanilla and salt.

Use immediately. Store any extra caramel sauce in the refrigerator, and gently reheat when you're ready for more deliciousness.

CHOCOLATE GANACHE

Makes ¾ cup

Ganache is one of the most simple, delicious things you can use to decorate a sweet treat. In its most liquid form, it can be drizzled on cupcakes or cakes; as it cools and thickens, it can used as a firmer dip for donuts or spread over a cheesecake, like our Chocolate Cheesecake (page 145). Try whipping some cooled ganache into a thick and rich chocolate frosting to smear between two Double Chocolate-Chip Cookies (page 93).

½ cup vegan semi-sweet chocolate chips

⅓ cup canned coconut milk

1 teaspoon melted coconut oil

Place the chocolate chips in a medium heatproof glass container.

In a small saucepan, bring the coconut milk and oil to a boil. Pour the hot mixture over top of the chocolate chips and let sit for 5 minutes before stirring. The ganache will thicken as it cools, so let it cool to the desired consistency before using.

Ganache may be stored in an airtight container in the refrigerator and reheated in a double boiler to soften up for use.

LEMON CURD

Makes 1 cup

Lemon curd is a thick, velvety cream with a fabulously tart yet sweet citrus flavour. You can use it in the Lemon Curd Tarts (page 185), like we do, as a spread for our scrumptious Lemon Blackberry Scones (page 33), or alongside an organic blueberry sauce with cornmeal waffles (page 25).

TIP: This curd will not be the bright yellow you might expect. If your heart is set on having it a lemon colour, add ¼ teaspoon turmeric or a bit of yellow food dye.

½ cup canned coconut milk

⅓ cup + 1 tablespoon organic sugar

⅓ cup + 1 tablespoon fresh lemon juice
   (about 2 or 3 lemons)

⅓ cup melted coconut oil

¼ cup water

⅛ teaspoon sea salt

2 tablespoons arrowroot starch

In a saucepan over medium heat, whisk together the coconut milk, sugar, lemon juice, oil, water, and salt. Warm for 2 to 3 minutes, whisking frequently. Add the arrowroot starch and, whisking constantly, cook the mixture for about 2 minutes, until it thickens to a custard-like consistency. (The whisk will make marks in the curd when thick enough.) Remove from the heat and let cool.

Transfer the curd to a Mason jar or other glass container and store it in the refrigerator for up to 2 weeks.

COCONUT WHIPPED CREAM

Makes ½ cup

Making whipped cream from coconut milk is so easy, I'm surprised that more people don't do it more often. There are many benefits of using coconut over dairy. Not only is coconut cream more flavourful, but it's also cholesterol-free and has medium-chain triglycerides, which our bodies absorb quickly and convert to energy, as opposed to storing as fat. This whipped cream is delicious on top of the Coconut Cream Pie (page 179) and really ramps up the Pumpkin Pie (page 195) if you add ¼ teaspoon cinnamon to it before spooning a giant dollop onto each slice.

1 can (400 mL) full-fat coconut milk, refrigerated right side up

⅔ cup organic powdered sugar, sifted

1 teaspoon vanilla extract

Without shaking, turn the can of coconut milk upside down and open the bottom—this is to make pouring easier. Pour off the liquid coconut milk, then gently scrape off any excess milk that remains on the cream. Spoon the remaining cream into a medium bowl and add the sugar. Using a hand mixer (my choice), or a fork or whisk, mix until incorporated. Gently fold in the vanilla.

Refrigerate overnight or for at least 3 hours before using. This whipped cream needs to be chilled, so be mindful when adding it to desserts you are taking with you to potlucks and the like.

ACKNOWLEDGEMENTS

....

Together, we would like to thank:

Our customers, who from day one have blogged, shared, and tweeted our business into the social phenomenon it has become. We never tire of seeing the smiles on the faces of people walking into Bunner's for the first time or of talking with our many cherished customers who have long since become friends.

Animal rights activists, for everything that you do to fight this uphill battle and for energizing us with your actions by reminding us why we love doing what we're doing.

All the like-minded businesses in our community, for offering us so much advice and feedback and for really inspiring us. (Go Toronto! What a great and vibrant city!)

Martin at Forever Interiors, for generously supplying us with an endless bounty of beautiful reclaimed wood backdrops.

Paul and Kira, for hosting our delicious breakfast shoot.

Jan, Gareth, and Erica, for sitting through so, so many shots.

Ben Quinn, for jumping in at the last second to help us out on our staff pic day.

Mrs. Huizenga's, for letting us use their super-hip, shabby-chic collection.

Sarah Baggio, for so kindly trusting us with her prized Pyrex collection.

Sherry Vanstone and Sam Rivait, our beautiful beauty team.

And last but in no way least, our editor, Kate Cassaday, and the entire HarperCollins crew, for their commitment to making this the absolute best book possible. Thank you for all your hard work, Kate and Co.!

Personal Acknowledgements

Thanks to . . .

Mom and Dad, for raising me to be an independent person, for giving me the freedom to make my own choices, and for always being proud of me and believing in me no matter what.

Our staff, for working so hard for us and for always being so fun and amazing. Every single one of you has helped make our business successful.

Amelia Earl and Nathalie Andrews—we couldn't have written this book without you. We will never be able to thank you enough for allowing us the freedom of time to do this and for being incredible bakers and pals.

To my 1 Middle Gang, Jon House, and Sabrina Marcantonio—my chosen family—thanks for being the best pals a girl could ever have and for never doubting (at least to my face) that opening a business was anything less than awesome. Love your guys' guts.

Laurie Rittinger, for being the original #1 fan.

Mark and Andy, for fostering my bossy nature and teaching me how to make my goals measurable.

Kevin, my sweetheart and business partner: How could I have been so lucky? Thank you for being my partner and walking this path beside me. I love you more each and every day that I know you. I'm so grateful for your impact on my life, for pushing me to do my best, for being there to celebrate with me, and for wiping my little tears of frustration away. Without you, Bunner's would still be a daydream. With you, it's a full-blown, awesome reality.

—A. W.

Thanks to . . .

Mom and Dad, for always supporting me, for encouraging me to do my best, for sharing your wisdom and experience, and for teaching me how to grow, adapt, and evolve with the trials of life—all with a sense of humour.

The team—the amazing staff of Bunner's, past and present—whose hard-working, hard-laughing dedication to getting the job done has brought us to where we are. You have humbled us countless times with your perseverance when the days were long and the work was stacked high.

Amelia, for taking the reins with quiet confidence and setting the benchmark for a new era of trust and confidence in management.

Nathalie, for your self-directed and tireless work ethic, pace setting, competence, and positive energy from day one.

My Higher Power, for the strength and courage to be of service.

Friendly Group, my second family, for their friendship, love, support, and strength.

Ashley, my Bun and partner: We've accomplished and overcome so much together. Thank you for all your hard work, creative passion, and inspiration; for sharing the good times and enduring the bad times (it's been a long road, and we've moved mountains); for always laughing at my cringe-worthy Jam-Irish accents and dad jokes; for all my attentions; and for making me my best self.

—K. M.

INDEX

agar-agar, 14

agave nectar, 16

almond milk, 16

almonds

    Rocky Road Cookies, 97

Amelia's "Seal the Deal" Pumpkin Scones, 35–36

apples

    Apple-Cinnamon Buckwheat Muffins, 53

    Apple Crisp, 197

    Apple Pie, 173

applesauce (in baking), 15

apricot jam

    Rugelach, 211

arrowroot starch, 14

Ashley's Delight Cake, 139–40

baking ingredients, 13–18

baking measurements, 9, 11, 18

baking tools and equipment, 10–12

bananas

    Ashley's Delight Cake, 139–40

    Banana Chocolate-Chip Muffins, 55

    Banana Date Scones, 31

    Banana Walnut Pancakes, 27

    Spiced Banana Rum Cookies, 205

bars and squares

    Blondies, 101

    Brownies, 99

    Chocolate Chip–Coconut Pretzel Bars, 105

    Date Squares, 107

    Mint Brownies, 99

    Nanaimo Bars, 103

    Peanut Butter Brownies, 99

    Walnut Brownies, 99

See also cookies

beet juice
    Red Velvet Cake, 133–34
Birthday Cake, 129
biscuits
    Herb and Garlic Biscuits, 71
    Spicy Cheddar Biscuits, 69
    See also scones
black beans
    Mexi Pockets, 75
blackberries
    Blackberry Peach Pie, 175
    Lemon Blackberry Scones, 33–34
    Lemon Curd Tarts, 185
Blondies, 101
blueberries
    Blueberry Cake, 137
    Blueberry Grunt, 187
    Blueberry Hand Pies, 177
    Lemon-Blueberry Corn Muffins, 49
    Lemon Curd Tarts, 185
Bob's Red Mill products, 13, 17
bread crumbs, gluten-free, 17
    Mac and Cheese, 83
    Savoury Holiday Stuffing, 215
brown rice flour, 13
Brownie-Caramel Chocolate Cheesecake, 146
Brownies, 99
buckwheat flour
    Apple-Cinnamon Buckwheat Muffins, 53
butter, non-hydrogenated vegan, 14–15
Butter Tarts, 181
"buttermilk," 15–16
Buttermilk Pancakes, 27

cakes
    to frost, 220–23
    Ashley's Delight Cake, 139–40
    Birthday Cake, 129
    Blueberry Cake, 137

cakes *(continued)*

    Chocolate Cake, 131

    Cookies and Cream Chocolate Cake, 131

    Jam Swirl Pound Cake, 143

    Josephine Louise Snack Cake, 134

    Mocha Cake, 131

    Pound Cake, 143

    Raspberry Cake, 137

    Red Velvet Cake, 133–34

    Strawberry Cake, 137

    See also cheesecakes; cupcakes

canola oil, 14

canola spray, 10

Caramel Buttercream Frosting, 159–60

Caramel Cupcakes, 159–60

Caramel Sauce, 239

carrots

    Gingerbread Carrot Muffins, 59

    Savoury Holiday Stuffing, 215

    Veggie Pot Pie, 79–80

cheese shreds, Daiya, 17

    Mac and Cheese, 83

    Mexi Pockets, 75

    Pizza, 85

    Pizza Pockets, 77

    Spicy Cheddar Biscuits, 69

cheesecakes

    Brownie-Caramel Chocolate Cheesecake, 146

    Chocolate Cheesecake, 145–46

    "Light" Chocolate Cheesecake, 146

    Pumpkin Cheesecake, 201

    Zebra Striped Cheesecake, 146

    See also cakes

cherries, maraschino

    Shortbread Cookies, 207

chocolate, 16–17

chocolate chips, vegan, 17

Cocoa Camino products, 16–17

cocoa powder, 16–17

Banana Chocolate-Chip Muffins, 55

Birthday Cake, 129

Blondies, 101

Brownie-Caramel Chocolate Cheesecake, 146

Brownies, 99

Chocolate Buttercream Frosting, 227

Chocolate Cake, 131

Chocolate Cheesecake, 145–46

Chocolate Chip Cookies, 91

Chocolate Chip Creamies, 91, 93

Chocolate Chip Granola, 29

Chocolate Chip–Coconut Pretzel Bars, 105

Chocolate Cupcakes, 153

Chocolate Ganache, 241

Chocolate-Glazed Donuts, 121

Chocolate Zucchini Muffins, 57

Cinnamon Chocolate Buttercream Frosting, 161–63

Cookies and Cream Chocolate Cake, 131

Double-Chocolate Chip Cookies, 93

Fauxstess Cupcakes, 153

Josephine Louise Snack Cake, 134

"Light" Chocolate Cheesecake, 146

Mexican Chocolate Cupcakes, 161–63

Mint Brownies, 99

Mocha Cake, 131

Nanaimo Bars, 103

Peanut Butter and Chocolate Chip Pancakes, 27

Peanut Butter Brownies, 99

Peppermint Bark, 213

Pumpkin Cheesecake, 201

Pumpkin Chocolate-Chip Muffins, 63

Red Velvet Cake, 133–34

Rocky Road Cookies, 97

chocolate *(continued)*

    Shortbread Cookies, 207

    S'more Cookies, 97

    Walnut Brownies, 99

    Zebra Striped Cheesecake, 146

Cinnamon Buns, 39–40

Cinnamon Chocolate Buttercream Frosting, 161–63

Cinnamon Sugar, 39–40, 117

Cinnamon Sugar Donuts, 117

Cocoa Camino products, 16–17

coconut, shredded

    Chocolate Chip–Coconut Pretzel Bars, 105

    Coconut Cream Pie, 179

    Lumberjack, The, 123

    Nanaimo Bars, 103

    Smoked Coconut Bacon, 123

    Supersonic Granola, 29

    Toasted Coconut Donuts, 119

coconut milk, 15

coconut milk beverage, 16

coconut oil, 14

Coconut Whipped Cream, 245

coconut yogurt, 15

    Pound Cake, 143

    Sugar Cookies, 209

coffee

    Mocha Cake, 131

confections

    Maple Fudge, 111

    Peppermint Bark, 213

cookies

    Chocolate Chip Cookies, 91

    Chocolate Chip Creamies, 91, 93

    Double Chocolate-Chip Cookies, 93

    Gingerbread Cookies, 203

    Oatmeal-Raisin Cookies, 95

Rocky Road Cookies, 97

Rugelach, 211

Shortbread Cookies, 207

S'more Cookies, 97

Spiced Banana Rum Cookies, 205

Sugar Cookies, 209

See also bars and squares

Cookies and Cream Chocolate Cake, 131

corn

Veggie Pot Pie, 79–80

cornmeal

Lemon-Blueberry Corn Muffins, 49

Sunday Morning Cornmeal Waffles, 25

cranberries, dried

Supersonic Granola, 29

Sweet Potato–Cranberry Muffins, 47

cranberries, fresh or frozen

Cranberry Pear Crisp, 199

cream cheese, Tofutti non-hydrogenated vegan

Chocolate Cheesecake, 145–46

Cream Cheese Frosting, 229

Pumpkin Cheesecake, 201

Rugelach, 211

Creamies, Chocolate Chip, 91, 93

cupcakes

Caramel Cupcakes, 159–60

Chocolate Cupcakes, 153

Fauxstess Cupcakes, 153

French Toast Cupcakes, 165

Ice Cream Sandwiches, 153

Lemon Cupcakes, 157

Mexican Chocolate Cupcakes, 161–63

Pumpkin Pie Cupcakes, 155

Vanilla Cupcakes, 155

See also cakes

custard powder, vegan

    Nanaimo Bars, 103

Daiya products, 17

dates

    Banana Date Scones, 31

    Date Squares, 107

desserts

    Apple Crisp, 197

    Blueberry Grunt, 187

    Cranberry Pear Crisp, 199

Donut Glaze, 237

donuts

    Chocolate-Glazed Donuts, 121

    Cinnamon Sugar Donuts, 117

    Lumberjack, The, 123

    Toasted Coconut Donuts, 119

Double Chocolate-Chip Cookies, 93

Earth Balance products, 14–15

egg substitutes, 15

fats and oils, 14–15

    butter and shortening, vegan non-hydrogenated, 14–15

    buttery spread, 15

    buttery sticks, 15

    canola oil, 14

    canola spray, 10

    grapeseed oil, 14

Fauxstess Cupcakes, 153

flavour extracts, 17

flour(s)

    all-purpose flour, gluten-free, 13

    brown rice flour, 13

    garbanzo and fava flour, 13

    varieties, 13

French Toast Cupcakes, 165

frostings
    to frost a cake, 220–23
    Caramel Buttercream Frosting, 159–60
    Caramel Sauce, 239
    Chocolate Buttercream Frosting, 227
    Chocolate Ganache, 241
    Cinnamon Chocolate Buttercream Frosting, 161–63
    Cream Cheese Frosting, 229
    Lemon Buttercream Frosting, 233
    Maple Buttercream Frosting, 235
    for Spiced Banana Rum Cookies, 205
    Strawberry-Jam Buttercream Frosting, 139–40
    Vanilla Buttercream Frosting, 225
    See also glazes, dips, and sauces

garbanzo and fava flour, 13
Gingerbread Carrot Muffins, 59
Gingerbread Cookies, 203
glazes, dips, and sauces
    for cinnamon buns, 39–40
    for scones, 33–34, 35–37
    Caramel Sauce, 239
    Chocolate Ganache, 241
    Cinnamon Sugar, 39–40, 117
    Coconut Whipped Cream, 245
    Donut Glaze, 237
    Lemon Curd, 243
    Maple Dip, 123
    Maple Nutmeg Glaze, 35–36
    Vanilla Dip, 119
    See also frostings
gluten-free (defined), 11
gluten-free products
    all-purpose flour, 13
    bread crumbs, 17

gluten-free products *(continued)*
    oats, 17
    pretzels, 105
granola
    Chocolate Chip Granola, 29
    Supersonic Granola, 29
grapeseed oil, 14

Herb and Garlic Biscuits, 71

Ice Cream Sandwiches, 153
ingredients (for baking), 13–18
    brand names, 15

Jam Swirl Pound Cake, 143
Josephine Louise Snack Cake, 134

Lemon Blackberry Scones, 33–34
Lemon-Blueberry Corn Muffins, 49
Lemon Buttercream Frosting, 233
Lemon Cupcakes, 157
Lemon Curd, 243
Lemon Curd Tarts, 185
Lemon Poppyseed Muffins, 61
"Light" Chocolate Cheesecake, 146
Lumberjack, The, 123

Mac and Cheese, 83
maple syrup
    Amelia's "Seal the Deal" Pumpkin Scones, 35–36
    Banana Date Scones, 31
    Lumberjack, The, 123
    Maple Buttercream Frosting, 235
    Maple Dip, 123
    Maple Fudge, 111
    Maple Nutmeg Glaze, 35–36

　　　Maple Plum Pie, 193

　　　Pumpkin Pie, 195

　　　Smoked Coconut Bacon, 123

marshmallows, vegan

　　　Rocky Road Cookies, 97

　　　S'more Cookies, 97

measurements

　　　cups and spoons for, 11

　　　equivalents for, 18

　　　importance of, 9

Mexi Pockets, 75

Mexican Chocolate Cupcakes, 161–63

milks, non-dairy

　　　almond milk, 16

　　　"buttermilk," 15–16

　　　coconut milk, 15

　　　rice milk, 15–16

　　　soy or coconut milk beverage, 16

Mint Brownies, 99

Mocha Cake, 131

muffins

　　　Apple-Cinnamon Buckwheat Muffins, 53

　　　Banana Chocolate-Chip Muffins, 55

　　　Chocolate Zucchini Muffins, 57

　　　Gingerbread Carrot Muffins, 59

　　　Lemon-Blueberry Corn Muffins, 49

　　　Lemon Poppyseed Muffins, 61

　　　Pumpkin Chocolate-Chip Muffins, 63

　　　Sweet Potato–Cranberry Muffins, 47

mushrooms

　　　Pizza, 85

　　　Pizza Pockets, 77

　　　Veggie Pot Pie, 79–80

Nanaimo Bars, 103

oats, gluten-free, 17
    Apple Crisp, 197
    Cranberry Pear Crisp, 199
oats, gluten-free *(continued)*
    Date Squares, 107
    Oatmeal-Raisin Cookies, 95
    Supersonic Granola, 29
olives
    Pizza, 85
    Pizza Pockets, 77
onions
    Pizza Pockets, 77
    Savoury Holiday Stuffing, 215
    Veggie Pot Pie, 79–80

pancakes and waffles
    Banana Walnut Pancakes, 27
    Buttermilk Pancakes, 27
    Peanut Butter and Chocolate Chip Pancakes, 27
    Sunday Morning Cornmeal Waffles, 25
pastry
    Savoury Pastry, 73
    Sweet Pastry, 171
    See also pies, tarts, and pastries
peaches
    Blackberry Peach Pie, 175
peanut butter
    Peanut Butter and Chocolate Chip Pancakes, 27
    Peanut Butter Brownies, 99
pears
    Cranberry Pear Crisp, 199
peas
    Veggie Pot Pie, 79–80
Peppermint Bark, 213
peppers, sweet bell and hot
    Mexi Pockets, 75

    Pizza, 85

    Pizza Pockets, 77

    Spicy Cheddar Biscuits, 69

pesto

    Pizza, 85

pies, tarts, and pastries

    Apple Pie, 173

    Blackberry Peach Pie, 175

    Blueberry Hand Pies, 177

    Butter Tarts, 181

    Coconut Cream Pie, 179

    Lemon Curd Tarts, 185

    Maple Plum Pie, 193

    Mexi Pockets, 75

    Pizza Pockets, 77

    Pumpkin Pie, 195

    Rugelach, 211

    See also pastry

pineapple

    Pizza Pockets, 77

Pizza, 85

Pizza Pockets, 77

plums

    Maple Plum Pie, 193

poppy seeds

    Lemon Poppyseed Muffins, 61

potato starch, 14

Pound Cake, 143

pretzels, gluten-free

    Chocolate Chip–Coconut Pretzel Bars, 105

pumpkin purée

    Amelia's "Seal the Deal" Pumpkin Scones, 35–36

    Gingerbread Carrot Muffins, 59

    Pumpkin Cheesecake, 201

    Pumpkin Chocolate-Chip Muffins, 63

    Pumpkin Pie, 195

pumpkin purée *(continued)*

    Pumpkin Pie Cupcakes, 155

raisins

    Butter Tarts, 181

    Oatmeal-Raisin Cookies, 95

    Rugelach, 211

raspberries

    Lemon Curd Tarts, 185

    Raspberry Brownies, 99

    Raspberry Cake, 137

Red Velvet Cake, 133–34

rice flour, brown, 13

rice milk, 15–16

rice pasta

    Mac and Cheese, 83

Rocky Road Cookies, 97

Rugelach, 211

salsa

    Mexi Pockets, 75

sauces. *See* glazes, dips, and sauces

Savoury Holiday Stuffing, 215

Savoury Pastry, 73

scones

    Amelia's "Seal the Deal" Pumpkin Scones, 35–36

    Banana Date Scones, 31

    Lemon Blackberry Scones, 33–34

    See also biscuits

Shortbread Cookies, 207

Smoked Coconut Bacon, 123

S'more Cookies, 97

soy creamer, 16

soy milk beverage, 16

Spectrum canola oil, 14

Spiced Banana Rum Cookies, 205

Spicy Cheddar Biscuits, 69

squares. *See* bars and squares

squash, butternut
    Mac and Cheese, 83
    Veggie Pot Pie, 79–80
starches and thickeners, 14
    agar-agar, 14
    arrowroot starch, 14
    potato starch, 14
    xanthan gum, 14
strawberries
    Lemon Curd Tarts, 185
    Strawberry-Jam Buttercream Frosting, 139–40
strawberry jam
    Strawberry Cake, 137
Sucanat, 16
sugar, organic, 16
Sugar Cookies, 209
Sunday Morning Cornmeal Waffles, 25
Supersonic Granola, 29
Sweet Pastry, 171
Sweet Potato–Cranberry Muffins, 47
sweeteners, 16
    agave nectar, 16
    Sucanat, 16
    sugar, organic, 16

Toasted Coconut Donuts, 119
tofu, silken, 18
    Coconut Cream Pie, 179
    "Light" Chocolate Cheesecake, 146
    Pound Cake, 143
tomato sauce
    Pizza, 85
    Pizza Pockets, 77

Vanilla Buttercream Frosting, 225

Vanilla Cupcakes, 155
Vanilla Dip, 119
vanilla extract, 17
vegan products
    cheese shreds, 17
    chocolate chips, 17
    custard powder, 103
    marshmallows, 97
    non-hydrogenated butter and shortening, 14–15
    white chocolate, 213
veganism (defined), 11
Veggie Pot Pie, 79–80

waffles. *See* pancakes and waffles
walnuts
    Banana Walnut Pancakes, 27
    Maple Fudge, 111
    Walnut Brownies, 99
Whipped Cream, Coconut, 245
white chocolate, vegan
    Peppermint Bark, 213
Wholesome Sweeteners, 16

xanthan gum, 14

yeast breads and buns
    Cinnamon Buns, 39–40
    Pizza, 85

Zebra Striped Cheesecake, 146
zucchini
    Chocolate Zucchini Muffins, 57